Eric Letendre's

BEST
DOG NOW!

Eric Letendre's

BEST
DOG NOW!

Eric R. Letendre

CONTENTS

INTRODUCTION
ERIC LETENDRE'S: BEST DOG NOW!...

I know a title like, "BEST DOG NOW!," is a big promise and you may be skeptical. Of course, a dog trainer like me would say that.

All the trainers on the internet, Facebook, YouTube, and on TV make big claims they can help train your dog, but after just a few minutes searching for dog training help, the new dog owner scratches his head and thinks:

"WOW! This dog training stuff is confusing!"

WHAT TO DO BEFORE YOU START TRAINING

"Relax, Take a deep breath."

I am going to help you. If this is your tenth dog or your first puppy, if your dog is ten years old or ten weeks old, if you have a pure bred Dandie Dinmont Terrier or a Heinz 57 mixed breed from down South, I can help you.

> *We have used Eric to train two dogs now, most recently a highly reactive young male that we hated to bring anywhere. Eric stopped the behavior in ten minutes and after two private sessions with Eric's own dog, our boy was in group classes, with 8-10 other dogs, acting perfectly calm. We can now take him anywhere and know that he isn't going to lunge and bark. Eric understands dogs, but probably more importantly, he understands people and knows what we are doing wrong! Even if you have had dogs your whole life, go see Eric. I guarantee you will learn something new! We can't thank him enough!*

PAM EVANS

Since 1995, I have helped thousands of people all over the SouthCoast, Rhode Island, and beyond train their dogs. And if there is one thing I have learned it is this: I am convinced that just about anyone can learn how to train their dog.

First, you took the step to contact and hire a dog trainer (thank you for choosing me). This one step put you in a very small club. A club I call the 4% club. According to a February 5th, 2015 Dogster.com article, less than 5% of dog owners take their dogs to a training class. American Pet Product Association National Pet Owners Survey reported 4% of dogs in America take a training class. This shows you are more committed than most dog owners. Commitment is always the first step to successfully doing anything.

Second, my own background and experience tells me just about anyone can do this. My early experiences with dogs were not good. The dogs we had growing up were not well trained and my first dog was hit by a car and killed in front of me. When I decided to become a dog trainer, I enrolled in a dog trainers' program at a school in Newington, CT. It was a course that taught you how to be a dog trainer. This was way back in 1993. The instructor for the course informed me that I did not have a natural talent for training dogs or dog owners.

Funny when you think about it now. My YouTube channel has 23,000 subscribers and over 13 million video views. I have written four dog training books available on Amazon, amassed thousands of followers on Facebook, and received over 100 five-star Google reviews. I am referred by veterinarians and dog professionals all over. I worked Security K9 for seven years in Hartford, CT, provided K9 Security for World Wide Plaza in New York City, served as an Animal Control Officer for three years in Fall River, MA, started the dog training program at the Potter League for Animals in Middletown, RI, and much more. Suffice it to say, you would be hard-pressed to find any dog trainer with as much hands-on and varied experience.

I share all this to reassure you, we can help YOU train your dog! You really can (and will in most cases) get fast results training your dog.

HERE ARE SOME GUIDELINES TO HELP GET YOU STARTED:

1. There's no need to feel intimidated or nervous training your dog. We will do everything we can to help you. Please let us know at any time if you have questions, problems, or concerns.

2. Do your best to set aside a few minutes to practice with your dog every day. Teaching your dog to do a behavior requires repetitions. I'll give you some more tips on how to make this easy later in this book.

3. Consistency is a major factor to success in dog training. We provide a lot of supporting materials to help make sure everyone in the house is on the same page.

All right! Let's begin...

CHAPTER ONE:

LETENDRE'S LEARNING LADDER

> *Eric is the best investment I made after I got my dog. He is patient, relaxed, informative, and very experienced. You won't be disappointed.*

STEVE SULLIVAN

We developed Letendre's Learning Ladder to help you understand the dog training process. It is important to remember our job is to teach you to train your dog. The better we can help you to be successful, the happier everyone will be. You, me, and your dog. Because a trained dog has a much better quality of life than an untrained dog. A dog that pulls on leash, won't come back when called, jumps, growls, and barks will have a much more limited life than a dog who listens to the owner.

The ladder covers the important steps you need to take and is a tool to refer to any time you are stumped, or have a question, or problem. I always tell everyone: "Look to the ladder." All your dog training questions can be answered by using the ladder. Let's get started...

Letendre's
LEARNING LADDER

Ladder Rung	Description
THE 4% CLUB	Less than 4% of dog owners in America take a training class. Just one class and you and your dog become members of this unique club.
TOOLS	Use the right tools to help your dog learn.
COMMUNICATION	You have to teach your dogs what to do and what NOT to do.
RELATIONSHIP	A structured relationship will help your dog learn to live with you.
DOG'S WELLBEING	The training methods are humane and developed to improve your dog's wellbeing. Included on this rung is your dog's physical and mental health.
MANAGEMENT	Management helps set your dog up for success.
ON YOUR TERMS	When your dog lives on your terms, you will have a much more enjoyable, peaceful relationship.

FIRST RUNG: ON YOUR TERMS

When a dog comes into your home, he needs to live **"On Your Terms."** Many dog owners end up living on the dog's terms. Just yesterday, I met with a very nice family and they told me how the kids can't eat a sandwich without the dog grabbing it out of their hands. They must eat with the dog behind a baby gate or in the crate. They are living on the dog's terms.

Dogs need to live on our terms for THREE MAJOR reasons:

1. Frustration: If you come home and your dog jumps on you as you walk through the door, if your dog nips at your pant legs after you walk in, if you had a long stressful day and you decide to make a sandwich and relax, you turn your back and your dog grabs the sandwich, you will be frustrated. It is not good to be in a constant state of frustration with your dog. Once your dog lives on your terms, frustration goes away.

2. Dog's Safety: Dogs (especially young ones) are on suicide missions. They will eat chocolate, chew on electrical cords, swallow rocks, and so on. Your job training your dog is to keep him safe. This is done by teaching your dog your terms. DON'T jump on the counters, DON'T eat rocks, DON'T chew the electrical cords, etc.

3. Your Safety: I have seen plenty of people injured by their dogs. I have seen dogs pull on leash so hard the owners were injured. I've seen dogs jump and knock people over, I've seen dogs become aggressive and bite. Dogs must live on our terms to keep us safe!

SECOND RUNG: MANAGEMENT

Management is an extremely important part of having a dog or puppy and there are different management tools to help you such as baby gates, crates, and x-pens. As your dog is learning your terms, you need to manage your dog's behavior. A dog in the crate can't get into trouble. Management helps you set your dog up for success. Management is not fun. Management is an inconvenience. Training will help you replace management.

THIRD RUNG: DOG'S WELL-BEING

Your dog's well-being is very important and includes how you treat your dog, what you feed your dog, proper vet care, and providing enough physical and mental stimulation. When it comes to training, I teach dog owners how to use positive and negative consequences. When you train a dog, you must use and apply reinforcement and punishment. Science confirms you must use both reinforcement and punishment to properly train a dog. We show you how to use both and will go into more detail about this in Chapter Two.

FOURTH RUNG: RELATIONSHIP

A structured relationship is important when you live with a dog. Your dog needs to understand you have all the status in the relationship. We structure the relationship by controlling the dog's basic needs. We have terms for the food, resting areas, how we play with the dog, and how we interact with him.

FIFTH RUNG: COMMUNICATION

When you train a dog, you are changing the dog's behavior. The dog does not always want to do what you want. Proper communication is required to train your dog. To increase behavior, you use reinforcement. To stop behaviors, you must use and apply punishment. We'll cover this in more detail in Chapter Three.

SIXTH RUNG: TOOLS

There are different tools available to help you train your dog. Leashes, collars, and crates are all tools used to help train your dog. We'll cover tools in detail throughout this book.

> *I cannot say enough about Eric and his method of training. I see such a change in Bentley and since training there is peace in the home. I felt overwhelmed and didn't know how to fix the problem. Eric gives you the tools you need and the issue we had with biting and jumping was fixed in one day. Thank you for everything! He truly is amazing!*

WENDY CABRAL

SEVENTH RUNG: 4% CLUB

I included the 4% Club because according to a February 5, 2015 Dogster.com article, less than 5% of dog owners take their dogs to a training class. American Pet Product Association National Pet Owner's Survey reported 4% of dogs in America take a training class. If you received this book as part of my training program, you are now in the 4% Club. Congratulations!

> *We adopted a dog from a shelter three years ago. He's an amazing animal but would bark at anything and would never stop. No matter what we did we couldn't get him to control his barking or charging people. We finally decided to try a dog trainer. We weren't expecting it to work but Eric promised us that he could get our dog to stop this behavior. Eric came to our house and in one session was able to train our pup. He now no longer yells at us. The best part is that his anxiety level has gone down tremendously. I am thrilled that we found Eric and will be calling him again if and when we adopt more dogs. I strongly recommend Eric for any doggie needs!!!*

NATHANIEL SCHUDRICH

CHAPTER TWO:
12 WAYS TO ESTABLISH LEADERSHIP WITHOUT FORCE OR HARSH METHODS

I highly recommend Eric Letendre's Dog Training School! Eric knows dogs, all dogs! I recently got a Basset Hound puppy and Eric immediately helped me curb some chewing and biting habits that were driving us all nuts at home, lol. He is a great puppy, but we are enjoying him so much more with the proper methods to train him. I'm so grateful to Eric and the school! Eric is patient and sits down and talks over all your concerns and answers all questions before any training begins. As things have come up (like with the recent thunderstorm), I'm able to ask Eric about my dog's behavior and Eric offers some good practices that I immediately put into place at home. I am SO glad that I brought my dog to Eric! If you have a puppy or an adult dog that needs some training or basic obedience, look no further than Eric's school! Thank you, Eric!

SUE DEMERS

Back in the early 1990s, I went to a school in Connecticut to become a *"Professional"* dog trainer. If I remember correctly, it was a 350-hour course, taught over five or six months. The school was run by a guy that went through police dog training in the 1950s.

Training has evolved from the 1950s, but back in the day, it was extremely harsh, and it was all based on the belief that dogs had a strict pecking order. Needless to say, the dog had to learn that you were the supreme leader and **ANY** unwanted behavior or resistance on the dog's part was severely punished with physical force. Rollovers, scruff shakes, choke chain corrections, and other physical methods were used to "teach" the dog that the human was the supreme leader and there was zero tolerance for any misbehavior on the dog's part.

Very flawed theory. Here is what is important to understand. Dogs are social. Dogs have different personalities. Some dogs are very dominant, some are submissive, and many are in the middle.

In recent years, dog trainers have started to disagree with each other over the whole "pack theory" and many are saying that it does not exist. All one must do is live with or watch a group of dogs interact with each other. I have lived with as many as five dogs in my house and have observed thousands of dogs in group settings.

I am convinced that dogs do respond to leadership and that as the dog owner, you need to establish leadership to deal with behavior problems, teach obedience, and maintain a good relationship with your dog in the house.

You can become the leader by following some steps which I am going to share with you in this chapter.

ERIC LETENDRE'S #1 TRUTH ABOUT LEADERSHIP
Leadership is established through patience and understanding, not force or harsh methods.

START EARLY

If there is one piece of advice I could give to dog owners it would be this: <u>Start training as soon as you get your pup.</u> Don't wait for problems to develop. Start socializing, start obedience training, and work on establishing leadership. This chapter will show you how to do it.

CONTROL FOOD

For dogs, we <u>NEED</u> to control their food for many different reasons; the main one is to teach your dog that you are in control. Feeding once or twice a day (instead of free feeding - leaving the bowl out all day) is a great way for your dog to learn that you control the resources.

Have your dog do a quick sit or down-stay before every meal. This one step will quickly reinforce your position as the leader.

CONTROL GAMES

I love playing poker and if there is one thing I've learned about playing poker, it is to always control yourself during the game. If you start getting emotional, if you lose control during the game, you are toast. This is extremely important to remember when you are establishing leadership with your dog. You must control **ALL** the games. Losing control during the game gives your dog the wrong signals.

For example: The **tug game** is very popular with dog owners.

Most dogs love to play this game and owners give their dogs the wrong signals when playing. If your dog is pulling on the tug toy and you let go, you are giving your dog the signal that he is stronger. Your dog has won the game.

This can lead to problems down the road because if your dog picks up something of value, something like a chicken bone, your dog will think he can defend it. If, on the other hand, you have always played tug making sure your dog releases the toy when you are finished playing, your dog will learn to release on command regardless of what he picks up.

CONTROL SLEEPING AREAS

I read an article not too long ago about sleep learning. Studies are being held to see if we can learn and absorb information while sleeping. I wish I had that in high school. It would also be great if our dogs could learn while they were sleeping.

There is one thing they can learn though regarding sleeping areas. Where your dog sleeps is very important and you should control the area.

I am **NOT** opposed to having dogs sleep on beds or furniture if the dog is not showing any signs of aggression. If your dog ever tried to protect his space on the bed or couch, he needs to automatically lose any privilege to sleep on the bed.

A few years back I was working with a couple that had a Springer Spaniel. The husband worked third shift and would come home around 8:00AM. Their dog would sleep on the bed with the wife every night and jump off the bed when hubby came home.

When the dog was about 14 months old, he started to give a little growl when papa came home. The growl became bad enough for them to contact me. I evaluated the dog, looked at the surroundings, and gave my suggestions.

I informed them that their dog **COULD NOT** sleep on the bed along with some other suggestions. The wife refused to listen to my advice and continued to let him sleep on the bed. The growling got worse. One day when the husband came home, the dog attacked him for trying to remove him from the bed. The husband needed medical attention and the wife finally decided to keep the dog off the bed.

If your dog ever gives you any signs of aggression on the bed, make sure you keep your dog off it. If your dog is already growling at you, leave a leash on so you can pick up the leash and remove your dog safely with the leash. **Do not reach in**

<u>and grab the dog if he is growling.</u> In my experience, the first places you see signs of aggression are with sleeping areas and around food.

A good practice to get into is to get your dog to move when he is sleeping to test the response. If I walk into a room and my dog is sleeping on the couch, I will walk over to the dog and instruct him to get off.

If my dog jumps off the couch, I know that I am still in the leadership position. I also do this if I am walking through a room and my dog is in the way. Instead of stepping over my dog or walking around him, I give the command to move. This teaches my dog that I am in the leadership position.

CONTROL SOCIAL CONTACT

It is important that your dog accepts handling on your part. A lot of dogs will growl or bite if their owners tries to touch them in certain places. It can take some time to build up the relationship to the point where you can pick up your dog's paw and trim the nails. It may take some time to brush your dog all over without him fussing and resisting. Follow the steps in this chapter and you'll be able to establish leadership and handle your dog better.

<u>ERIC LETENDRE'S #2 TRUTH ABOUT LEADERSHIP</u>
Control the resources, control the dog.

DOWN-STAY

A down-stay is one of the best ways to develop leadership. I recommend doing two or three down-stays every day. The down-stay should last anywhere from three to ten minutes. You can do the down-stay with your dog while watching TV.

I once had a dog that came to live with me because he was having some behavior problems. I taught the dog down and then the stay command. Every day I would have this dog do down-stays while I was watching TV or working on the computer. Just this alone was enough to help the dog. I didn't have to do a lot of other training because the dog responded so well to the down-stay exercises.

FORMAL EYE CONTACT

In my library, I have a book titled: *"The Power of Eye Contact: Your Secret for Success in Business, Love, and Life,"* by Michael Ellsberg.

The description for the book states: *"Eye contact can land you a job. It can get you a date. It can deepen your connections with the people you love. It can make or break business relationships. It can help win a fight. It can win over an audience."*

It can also improve the relationship between you and your dog by helping you establish leadership and increase bonding. Eye contact is very interesting when it comes to dogs. Dogs use eye contact much the same way humans do. Dogs use eye contact to gain control over other dogs.

Think of your mother when you were a kid, looking at you across the room when you were misbehaving. A submissive dog, like an insecure person, will have a hard time holding eye contact. Staring at a strange person, like staring at a strange dog, could provoke a confrontation. Making eye contact with your dog can improve the bond and put you in the top spot. I recommend doing some eye contact sessions every day.

A good time to do it is when you feed your dog. As you put the bowl on the ground, have your dog do a stay command and look into your eyes. Have your dog hold eye contact for three to five seconds before you release your dog and let him eat. The stay and eye contact will greatly help you establish the lead position.

ERIC LETENDRE'S #3 TRUTH ABOUT LEADERSHIP
The only good dog is a tired dog. Establishing leadership is difficult, if not impossible, with a dog that has too much pent-up energy.

EXERCISE

"If it weren't for the fact that the TV set and the refrigerator are so far apart, some of us wouldn't get any exercise at all."

Joey Adams

One of my favorite quotes is: *"The only good dog is a tired dog."* This is very true for anyone that has a dog that is displaying behavior problems. Exercise is more like a side dish when it comes to the whole, "Becoming the Leader," program. You see, a dog with a lot of pent up energy is going to have problems. All the leadership, behavior, and obedience training in the world are not going to overcome energy problems.

Walking is a great way to exercise your dog. I walk my dog three miles every day and it is a great way for all of us to get the exercise. I highly recommend walking, but I also think it is important for your dog to run, to get all eight cylinders going, and to really go beyond aerobic. I am talking about having your dog run full speed for short bursts. I do not think it is a good idea for dogs to run for long sustained periods of time.

Let me explain: If you study most animals, you'll see that very few run for long periods of time. Most animals, especially carnivores, will run for very short bursts. A lion or tiger will turn it on, full speed, to catch his prey. The same is true for wolves. They try to catch their prey without expending all their energy. I found that my dogs were much more relaxed and in greater shape when I started to exercise them this way.

If your dog loves to retrieve it will be much easier to do this. I use a ball, Frisbee, or my favorite, the "Chuck it." The Chuck It is a stick with a plastic ball holder at the end. It allows you to pick up the ball without bending over, but more importantly, you can send the ball a long distance with a flick of the wrist.

By doing this on a regular basis, it will be much easier for you to live with your dog and much easier for your dog to live with you.

DIET

All kidding aside, I consider diet another "side dish" included with this chapter. What you feed your dog has a **HUGE** effect on how your dog behaves. I have seen big improvements in a dog's behavior once the diet was changed.

Most of the food that is produced and fed to our dogs is real garbage. It's cheaply made, with low-cost animal and vegetable by-products. If that is not bad enough, it is processed with preservatives, colorings, dyes, and dangerous chemicals like BHA and BHT.

Look at how our dog's health is quickly becoming as bad as ours. Cancer, diabetes, allergies, skin and coat problems, and a whole host of other ailments are cropping up.

A dog that is not feeling good will develop behavior problems. All the behavior and obedience training in the world will not help a dog that is sick from the diet that is being fed to him.

There are many opinions, beliefs, and theories about the best way to feed your dog. Personally, I follow the diet put forth by Dr. Ian Billinghurst. Here is his website if you'd like to learn more: http://www.barfworld.com/

STROKING, PETTING, FONDLING

My mom adopted a cockapoo when I was about 14 years old. His name was Toby and he was one of the worst behaved dogs. Housetraining issues, barking, chewing, and some other problems were just the tip of the iceberg.

I tried training him but he only liked one person - my mother. He would growl and bark at me. When I put him on leash about the only thing I could do was take him for a walk. You also have to remember; at the time I was not yet the Amazing Dog Training Man. I was 14 years old with very limited dog training experience.

My mother spent hours petting and stroking Toby. Looking back, Toby was practically addicted to my mother's touch. He would wait for her all day and when he would act up and bark or growl, she would try to calm him through petting and stroking. The problem was that she reinforced the bad behaviors.

My advice:
This advice would apply more to problem dogs.

<u>First</u>: I would stop petting for long periods of time. Petting would be reduced to quick pats and scratching for less than five seconds.

<u>Second</u>: The dog starts working for petting. Pet your dog after he has performed a quick command. It could be a sit, down, or something as simple as, "Give me your paw."

<u>Third</u>: NO petting when it is demanded. A lot of dogs demand that their owners pet and pay attention to them. I've seen dogs paw and bark at their owners for attention. If this happens, immediately have your dog do a command.

TOYS

I once worked with a client that was having leadership issues with her dog. I arrived at her house and was brought into a room with a floor that was covered with toys. I assumed she had three or four kids by the number of toys on the floor. I asked her how many kids she had. She gave me a puzzled look and said she didn't have any children. I looked around and asked: *"All these toys are your dog's?"*

Not only did her dog have all the toys, the room was also his. When I instructed her to take all the toys away except one, she almost fainted. I added that her dog could have his toys back once his behavior changed. It took me awhile, but she eventually did what I asked, and her dog's behavior changed quickly.

The easiest way to establish leadership is to control resources: food, games, sleeping areas, social contact, and toys. If your dog wants it, you need to control it. The lady I talked about above felt bad taking his toys away. I explained her dog already gets free room and board, has a great health care plan, receives loads of attention, and food and treats. There's no reason to feel bad and her dog must learn his proper place in the household.

When you take the toys away, use them to teach your dog that you are the leader and for obedience training. As your dog learns that you are the leader, more toys can be introduced.

ERIC LETENDRE'S #4 TRUTH ABOUT LEADERSHIP
Games are a great way to establish leadership. Control the game, control the dog.

PLAY MORE TUG

In the dog training world which I live in, there are a lot of opinions, theories, studies, and arguments about a lot of topics. One topic which gets everyone's panties in a bunch is tug-o-war. One school advises to never, under any circumstance, play tug. They claim tug is violent and teaches your dog to bite hard and will lead to aggressive behavior.

I find this view kind of interesting. Did you know that in the great country of England, there is a Tug-O-War Association? Their website states: *"Tug of War is a true noncontact competitive sport suitable for a wide range of abilities."*

Tug is a great noncontact game that you can play with your dog. I like that because dogs have a physical and psychological need to use their teeth and jaws. By playing tug, you can safely let your dog fulfill his need and teach him that you are the leader at the same time.

If you decide to play tug, you need to follow some rules:

First: Always start the game.

Second: Only use one tug toy that you keep separate from the others.

Third: Have your dog perform commands before, during, and after the tug game.

Fourth: If your dog's teeth get too close to your hands, immediately give your dog the command to release the toy.

Fifth: <u>YOU END THE GAME.</u> When you are finished playing the game, give your dog the command to release, have your dog do a down-stay, and put the toy away.

FORMAL TRAINING SESSIONS

"Dogs like to obey. It gives them security." James Herriot

Have you ever read any of James Herriot's books? He was an English country vet that wrote about his adventures. Great stuff and you won't be disappointed. His quote above is profound.

More dogs are put to sleep every year because of behavior problems than for any other reason. Obedience training does not have to be a long, labor intensive process. You really can train your dog in short, ten-minutes sessions. If you only have time to do one short session a day, you will see results. If you need to work on leadership, I recommend at least two formal training sessions done at different times during the day.

Leadership is essential when you have a dog in your house. Your dog will be more secure, and you'll have a safer dog.

<u>Final Words:</u> I think Jon Maxwell sums it up best: "*Leadership is influence.*" Once leadership is established, it is much easier

to train your dog and to stop behavior problems. Leadership truly is influence.

When we brought home our new puppy, she was a 4.5 pound ball of fluff, and teeth, and attitude! Although she has always been good with us, she very quickly demonstrated the hyper reactivity and forward aggression (an attempt to control the world around her) that is typical of her breed, but it was extreme. We were devastated, as we were sure it meant we would lose her. Eric not only demonstrated patience and confidence with her, but he helped my sons and me develop the understanding of her behavior and the training principles needed to help her grow into the wonderful dog we know she was meant to be. She is still young, but every day, every class we attend, she improves!

I enthusiastically recommend him to everyone I know. He is kind, funny, and what he teaches works. He doesn't teach you how to bully your dog into behaving, but rather he teaches you to become your dog's alpha through developing confidence in yourself and showing them affection and love with proper boundaries and conscious rewards. He explains the difference between what you THINK you are teaching them and what you are ACTUALLY teaching them. Thank you, Eric! Our puppy started as a tiny, terrible monster, and is becoming a gorgeous, loving, happy member of our "pack" and we now receive compliments on how much she is improving from our neighbors.

TRACY NUN

CHAPTER THREE:

WHY YOU NEED A SYSTEM TO TRAIN YOUR DOG

"Every system is perfectly designed to get the results it gets."

Donald Berwick

I met Eric through a friend, and I brought my two pups to meet him. Eric is a pleasure to talk to. I told him some of my concerns and what I was looking to accomplish. We started his class about two weeks later. Our first class was a one on one with both pups. During that meeting, he already had stopped my dogs from doing two of my biggest concerns; constant barking and learning the command NO. Every week in class, my dogs learned new commands with ease because Eric explains what to do and how to apply that command. Eric, in my opinion, is worth his weight in gold and I am looking forward to doing follow up classes with him. His place of training is 30 minutes from us and we probably pass dozen of trainers along the way, but I would definitely do it all again

SCOTT WESTCOAT

When you train a dog, you need to understand that dogs do two behaviors. They do what we call good behavior and bad behavior. A more accurate term would be acceptable and unacceptable behavior. We can list what we would call good behaviors, examples would be: sit, down, stay, come, etc. On the flip side we have what we would call "bad" behavior, jumping, excessive barking, chewing, nipping, begging, etc.

When you want your dog to DO a behavior you use reinforcement. Reinforcement increases behavior. When you want your dog to STOP doing a behavior you need to apply punishment.

My job is to show you how to use reinforcement to INCREASE behaviors and how to use punishment to STOP behaviors.

The system we developed is to associate words with reinforcement and punishment. We teach **GOOD, YES, WRONG, and NO.** Dog training is all about communication. For your dog to listen to you, you must establish a communication "system." Much the same way if you went to France you would only be able to communicate with French citizens that spoke English. Once you learned their language or "system" for speaking and writing, communication would be easier, and frustration would end.

We tend to get frustrated with our dogs because we do not effectively communicate with them. In this chapter, you'll learn how to get your dog to do what you want, when you want, by learning and teaching them a language you both understand.

Let's get started:

The words your dog will learn are:

1. GOOD (Duration)
2. YES (Release)
3. WRONG (Try Again)
4. NO (STOP)

The four words listed above will help you to teach your dog any command or trick. Once your dog understands the above four words, you have established a language or "communication system" between you and your dog and teaching sit, down, stay, come, heel, or fetch me a beer from the fridge will become much easier.

First, we need to have a quick lesson from a Russian physiologist by the name of Ivan Pavlov. Long story short, ole Ivan is famous for his work with dogs and what is referred to as Classical Conditioning.

Many are familiar with the story of his dogs hearing a bell and then getting food. The sound of the bell was paired with food. Within a short period of time, the dog would salivate just hearing the bell. The bell had no meaning until it was repeatedly paired with the food. This is known as Classical Conditioning.

This is important for us because we need to teach your dog **MARKERS**. A marker communicates important information to your dog. We'll use markers to let your dog know if he has successfully completed the command (YES), if he has made a mistake (WRONG), if you want your dog to continue what he is doing (GOOD), or if you want him to STOP doing a behavior (NO).

Dog training requires crackerjack timing, or the dog gets confused. Once confusion sets in, training becomes difficult, frustrating, and both the dog and owner want to quit. We must avoid that situation so to make training easy, we teach and work with markers.

TEACHING GOOD & YES

We are going to use Classical Conditioning by pairing these two words with food, much the same way Ivan did with the bell. We are going to give the words, **GOOD** and **YES**, meaning to your dog. We are going to "charge" the words **GOOD** and **YES** by pairing them with food.

GOOD

We want the word GOOD to mean "keep doing what you are doing." For example, if your dog was sitting politely by your side and you wanted him to stay in that position, you would say, "GOOD," and that would communicate to your dog... "keep doing what you are doing."

To teach this we will say, "GOOD," and then we will deliver the reward (a bite of your dog's food or a treat) to him. **It is very important that you GO TO YOUR DOG to deliver the reward.** Remember, you want your dog to continue the behavior so **DO NOT** let him get up and move toward you to get the food. **BRING THE FOOD TO HIM.**

Start off with some treats in your hand. It is important to understand that we are NOT asking your dog to do anything in particular at this point. We are just giving the word GOOD meaning to your dog. When you say the word GOOD, you are going to quickly reach in and give your dog a treat.

For the first few sessions, you'll just say your dog's name and once you get any attention you will say, "GOOD," and give the reward.

YES

We want the word YES to mean "you have successfully completed the command, your work here is done, you may go about your business." YES ends the behavior you were asking for. When you say, YES, the dog is released from the command. When you are teaching the word YES to your dog, **you will have him COME TO YOU to get the reward.**

Be enthusiastic when you say, YES! Use your voice and body language to get your dog to come over to you for the reward. Your dog should be excited when you say, YES!

You will use your dog's breakfast and dinner to teach him GOOD and YES. Start your feeding session with your dog in front of you. Say GOOD and deliver the food, GOOD and deliver the food, GOOD and deliver the food, YES and have your dog get up and come to you to get the food. Keep repeating with variability between GOOD and YES until your dog's meal is complete. This will give your dog enough repetitions for the words to start to have meaning. Once they have meaning, you can use them to train your dog.

EXAMPLE: You ask for a sit. Your dog sits and you say, GOOD, and deliver the reward to your dog. You would continue to say GOOD and reward. Your dog is learning to hold the command. Once you say YES, your dog is released from the command and comes to you to get the reward. Every command has a beginning and end. If you ask your dog to SIT, he should remain sitting until released... YES!

Make sense? Please let me know if you have questions about this. This step **CANNOT** be skipped. It is extremely important for the rest of your dog's training.

TEACHING WRONG

When training a dog to do obedience, there are times (especially in the beginning) when your dog will not do the command or will do a different behavior than you asked. In the early stages of training, **you do NOT want to apply any kind of correction.**

Giving your dog a correction too early in training will result in your dog getting nervous about training and you may suppress your dog's willingness to perform the commands in the future.

When your dog does not perform the command, you do not want to keep repeating it. You want to let your dog know he made a mistake without hurting his performance. When your dog does not correctly complete the command, you are going to simply say, WRONG, and turn away from your dog.

Often when a dog does not perform a command it is because he is confused, distracted, or not properly motivated. After you turn away from your dog, you'll get him engaged and his attention back on you to try again. <u>It is important to remember that your dog ONLY gets the reward (GOOD or YES) when the</u> <u>command is done correctly</u>.

TEACHING NO!

Dog training is split up into two parts. Teaching our dogs to do certain behaviors for us - sit, down, stand, come, etc. And teaching our dogs to STOP doing certain behaviors - jumping, chewing, barking, digging, etc.

The problem with teaching NO is that most people do not apply a negative consequence with the word. If a negative consequence is associated with the word NO, it is often not efficient or confuses the dog. The word NO must be associated with a negative consequence for your dog to stop doing certain unacceptable behaviors.

Once your dog has been punished, we always give the opportunity to do the behavior again. We want to END with your dog doing the correct behavior, so we can finish by REWARDING your dog. We never, ever end a training session on a negative note. We always end with your dog being successful and his tail wagging.

The goal is to teach your dog NO quickly. We want to only use a negative consequence a few times. Once the word NO has been associated with a negative consequence, just saying the word NO should be enough to stop the behavior.

You can watch our video "4 Words Every Dog Needs to Learn" on YouTube. Here is the link:

https://www.youtube.com/watch?v=G_-nLXdB5VM

Eric Letendre's dog training is the best! I got everything I was promised and more. He told me my ten-month old Boerboel, who was lacking some manners, would no longer have that problem when we were done training. I believed him because he is an honorable person... but I didn't really think it would be THAT FAST. Training and knowledge given is unbeatable. Eric, you have made me and Max much wiser and happier. Look no further if you are looking for training!

CHRISTINA WHEELER

CHAPTER FOUR:
TEACHING COME WHEN CALLED

DEFINITION OF COME WHEN CALLED

Come when called is when the dog immediately moves toward the owner as he calls the dog. The dog should move to the owner regardless of distractions or environment. The owner should have control over the dog when he gets to him. The dog should stay with the owner until released, given another command, or put on leash.

We have had three dogs and our current dog (a rescue) Jasper is the first one to be trained and we couldn't be happier with the results. Had we known what a difference training with Eric would have made, we most certainly would have had the other two dogs trained. Jasper went from a dog who jumped on people and pulled while walking to the point of choking to a dog that doesn't jump on people and can go on walks without a leash! It's been a freeing experience for both Jasper and our family. If you are considering training for your dog, we highly recommend Eric.

DAVE BOSWELL

Does Your Dog Ignore the Come When Called Command?

Quiz time: The best way to teach your dog to come when called is to use?

Everyone that said "Positive Reinforcement" can come to the front of the class and get a gold star. You correctly answered the question.

You need to reinforce and reward your dog for coming to you. But, the overwhelming majority of people that I work with use punishment and there is a good chance you are (GASP) doing the same thing. There is a strong chance that you are punishing your dog for coming to you and you don't even know it.

Let me explain with this quick story: A few years back I used to help people in the pet industry. I would help them with their business. I worked with pet groomers, dog trainers, and dog day cares.

Anyway, I was coaching this one person and within a few weeks I couldn't stand it. I would see her number pop up on my cell phone and I would cringe. Within a few days I started to avoid her calls. See, every time she called it was one long, continuous, one sided conversation about everything that was bad in her life - which was considerable. She complained about her business, her customers, her dogs, her back, her husband, the town she lived in... it went on and on and I COULDN'T STAND TALKING TO HER.

It was punishment just seeing her name on my cell phone so I would avoid her calls as long as I could and eventually sent her money back and ended the relationship.

Which brings us to your dog and avoiding your call.

If you call your dog over to you and you immediately put him on leash, you have just effectively punished him for coming. You didn't punish intentionally but the principles of behavior work like gravity. You can jump or trip off your roof. Either way - the result is going to be the same.

The best way to teach your dog to come when called is to set your dog up to successfully complete the command. Reward your dog for coming and then repeat the process. That's just one of the secrets I show dog owners to get better results. Understanding this, let me give you step-by-step instructions on teaching the come when called command.

Here is a transcript of a recent COME WHEN CALLED class I taught.

Today we are going to be teaching your dog to COME WHEN CALLED. This is an extremely important command and we want to make sure your dog learns this one. This is truly a life-saving command. If your dogs do not COME WHEN CALLED, they could get lost, injured, or killed so we are going to break this command down step-by-step to make sure you get great results.

Before we start, quick show of hands. How many of your dogs come when called?

Okay, so our dogs are all over the place, some are good, some not so good. It does not matter. I just wanted to see where we are with this command. So, there are some steps we need to follow when teaching this command. Here is what you need to know.

First, we need to teach the dog the word COME means to move towards you. Second, for your dog to get good at COMING WHEN CALLED, your dog needs to develop a sense of freedom. Third, you must be careful of UNINTENTIONAL PUNISHMENT, and finally we need the dog to learn to COME to you when distracted. So, let's get started.

The first exercise I like to do is called the Restrained Recall. When you hear me saying recall I am referring to COME WHEN CALLED. The Restrained Recall Exercise is a great one to start with. I like teaching this because it sets your dog up for success. Often, when it comes to the recall command, the dog is set up for failure. For example, your dog is 20 feet away from you when you call COME. The dog is interested in some scent or looking at something else and ignores you.

You call COME and your dog does not respond. You call it again, COME, COME, COME HERE, COME OVER HERE!!! Your dog continues to ignore you. Your dog is also learning to ignore the command. This is why we start with the Restrained Recall to set your dog up for success.

The exercise is done with two people. The first person holds onto the leash. The second person walks up to the dog and gets him excited. You want your dog to be super excited when you do this. Once your dog is excited, you quickly move away from your dog. You want your dog looking at you when you do this. As you run 15 to 20 feet away, you want your dog to be straining on the leash. You want your dog pulling on the leash trying to get to you. This is setting up your dog for success.

Once you are 20 feet away you will face your dog. At this point you will clearly say your dog's name, SPARKY! The first person will drop the leash and as your dog is running to you, you will say COME!

When your dog gets to you, reach down, take your dog's collar, tell him GOOD, and give the dog a treat. The reason I want you to grab the collar is simple. You see, when you call your dog there a few things he will do. First, some dogs will do what we call drivebys. A driveby is when you call your dog and he comes racing at you 30 miles an hour and goes by you at 30 miles an hour. The second thing a dog will do is play keep away. They get close to you but won't let you get them. It is common for a lot of dogs to play keep away.

And lastly, some dogs hate getting their collars grabbed. There are a lot of negative associations with the collar. Often when a dog gets into trouble, the collar is grabbed. The dog is in the garbage, "GET OUT OF THERE," your dog jumps on someone, "GET OFF," they are on the counter, "GET OVER HERE," and the collar is grabbed. We want to change this and make collar grabs a positive experience.

Quick recap, first person holds onto the leash. Second person get the dog excited and runs away. Around 15 to 20 feet away, face the dog and clearly say the dog's name, SPARKY! The first person drops the leash. As the dog starts running towards you, the second person will say COME! When the dog gets to you, reach out and take the collar and then say good and reward. Excellent, any questions? Let's try it out.

Okay, so that is the restrained recall. That exercise does take two people, but it is great to do because it is fun and sets the dog up for success. The next thing we need to do is teach your dog to move towards you when you say COME! The funny thing is most of your dogs already know the command COME. They just choose when they are going to do it. The biggest problem is when there is a distraction.

Your dog is in the backyard, you call COME, and your dog ignores you. You need your dog to learn to leave the distraction and come to you. You need to influence the dog's behavior and get him to follow through with the command. This is done with a long line.

With the long line, you will be able to influence your dog's behavior from a distance. So, if your dog is 20 feet away, you would say COME. If your dog does not move towards you, the long line is used to get your dog to come to you.

Here is how you use the long line. You would say your dog's name and then the command: SPARKY, COME. If your dog does not respond to you, take the line and give it a slight pop and back up as your dog moves towards you. The movement is important. If you do not move backwards as you call your dog, you'll end up dragging your dog. We want your dog moving to you and the backwards movement is what will get him to come to you. Let me show you.

Okay, it's important to remember that dogs are attracted to movement. The movement is what draws the dog into you. You need to tug on the leash and move backwards at the same time. Draw the dog into you, don't reel the dog in like a fish. When your dog gets to you, reward your dog. Now you try it out.

I strongly recommend everyone get a long line to practice with your dog. The long line will help you get the dog to do the command. Without the long line, your dog will learn to ignore you. I always put this on when I go the beach or hiking with my dog. With the long line attached, I can always make sure my dog will come when called.

Does that make sense to everyone? Does anyone have a question? When I use the long line, I use it as a drag line. I let my dog drag it behind him and I stay close to the line. If my dog sees another dog or person and starts to run to him, I can step on the line and prevent it. If I call my dog and he does not respond, I pick up the line and use it to get my dog to come when I call.

So, we start off with the restrained recall, we then use the long line to get 100% compliance with the recall. The other thing you need to be aware of is punishment. Remember, reinforcement increases behavior and punishment decreases or eliminates behavior. So, we must be careful about punishing our dogs for coming to us. You see, dogs are often punished by the owner and the owner does not even realize it.

Think about this. I was once out with a friend and his new puppy. We went to the beach and went for a 45-minute walk. My friend is a real nice guy but does not like advice of any kind. You know the type; they know how to do everything and need no help. So, I never give this guy any dog training advice. We're walking down the beach and after 45 minutes or so we head back towards our car. Right before my friend was about to call his puppy, I asked him if I could give him some advice on coming when called. He held up his hand and said: "Naw, I'm good. My pup is doing fine." "Okay," I said and clammed up as my friend called his puppy to him.

I knew he was about to make a giant mistake, but I didn't say a word. He called his puppy to him. His puppy came racing to him and the second his puppy got to him he punished his pup. Now, he did it unintentionally, but intentional and unintentional punishment work the same. You see, his puppy was running around having a great time. His puppy was playing in the sand dunes, splashing in the water, sniffing dead fish carcasses, all the stuff puppies love. When he called the puppy and he came running over, my friend reached down and slapped the leash on his puppy.

And in that split second, he punished the pup. His puppy was off leash, having fun, running around and then he went to the owner, my friend. My friend put the leash on and that was the punishment. The second the leash goes on what happened? Fun was over, freedom was taken away. Game over. The dog remembers this. I know the next time my friend lets his puppy off leash his pup won't come back to him because what will the pup remember? The pup will remember, "This is the guy who put me on leash when I came to him."

So, we must be careful about punishment when calling our dogs. The next question I get is, "How do I ever leave the beach?" Simple. With the drag line on, when it is time to go you simply step on the leash, pick it up and walk back to your car. You don't associate the command COME with you putting the dog on leash. Make sense? Great, let's try it again.

Okay, now the next exercise I like to do is one where the dog learns to move away from me. You see, we think it is good for a dog to learn to move towards you and to move away from you. We teach the dog to GO and COME. We want to control the direction of the dog.

It can be difficult for a dog to learn to move away from you, but we'll show you an easy way to do this. You may be wondering why we would have to teach the dog to move away. Dogs like to crowd us, they crowd us around the door, when we're cooking, and when people come to visit. These are all good times to have your dog move away from you. Also, think about when you call your dog to you. There are times when the dog should move away from you instead of moving to you. For example, if your dog was loose and on the other side of Route 6, you may not want to call your dog to you. You may want your dog to move away from you. Calling your dog could call him into the path of a car.

This is why we want to control the direction of our dogs. We want them to go and to come towards us. The good news is it is very easy to teach this, and it is fun to teach. The way we teach it is to give the dog a target to go to. I use a paper plate because it gives the dog a clear target to move towards. This is good if you were practicing on grass. We put the paper plate on the ground and put a treat in the middle of the plate. We hold the dog back by his flat collar. You hold the dog back and then say GO. Your dog runs out to get the treat and once he has gotten the treat, you can now say COME and call your dog back to you. So, you can send your dog out - GO and call your dog back to you - COME. Let me show you.

Okay, now it's your turn. Use the plate as the target and make sure your dog sees you put the treat on the plate. After you practice this your dog will learn to move away from you when you say GO. Go ahead and try it with your dog and I'll come around and see how you are doing.

Excellent. Everyone is doing a great job. You want to practice outside, from longer and longer distances, and have fun doing it. So, we do the RESTRAINED RECALL exercise, we work your dog on the LONG LINE, we train the RECALL around distractions, we do the PAPER PLATE RECALL, and there is one last thing I want you to know and understand.

Imagine for a second you have a guest come over and your dog bolts out the front door. Your dog is heading for the street. What would you say to your dog as he is running towards the street? Anyone? Any idea?

If it was my dog and he was running towards the street I would yell out NO! You see, in this situation we would think COME would be the command but remember this, your dog is running away from you. What do you want the dog to do as he is running away from you? YES! You want your dog to STOP! You want your dog to stop running away. What word has your dog learned that means STOP? NO means STOP! This is why teaching your dog NO is so important. NO means STOP what you are doing. Once your dog stops you can then call your dog back to you with COME.

NO is such an important word for your dog to learn because you often must STOP a behavior before you ask for a behavior. For example, your dog jumps on somewhen when they walk into your house. I would not tell me dog to SIT. I would say NO to stop the behavior, then I would say SIT. Does that make sense?

It is very sad there is such an anti-punishment movement in dog training right now because NO really does save the dog's life. I have worked with dogs that swallowed rocks, chased cars, chewed on electrical cords. NO paired with punishment is what stopped the behavior and saved the dog's life. Okay, any questions? Comments? Concerns? Excellent, work recalls this week and I'll be here to answer any questions. Great group of dogs. Thank you!

These Seven Tips Will Help Your Dog Come When Called - Especially the Sixth One

Got a question the other day. Here it is:

"Eric, we got snow the other day and now my dog won't come back when I call him. Is there anything I can do?"

If I couldn't answer this question, I'd be what the French call: "Les Incompétents." Since I'm NOT incompetent (at least not when it comes to dog training) let me share seven tips to get your dog to come when called:

1. <u>Make yourself more interesting</u>. Use your voice and body language to get your dog interested in what you are doing. Movement helps big time.

2. <u>Use a long line for a few days</u>. Dog training is all about influence. When your dog is off-leash, you only have your voice to influence your dog. If you need more than your voice, attach a long line and use it to guide your dog to you.

3. <u>Increase the reward</u>. Want me to do something for you? Get the right reward and you'll get the right behavior.

4. <u>Back to basics</u>. Go back to doing the Restrained Recall Exercise that I talked about earlier in this chapter.

5. <u>Work on attention</u>. Chances are if your dog is not paying attention to you, your dog will not come back to you.

6. <u>Make it a game</u>. If I could only share one secret to the recall command with you it'd be this one. Make coming when called a game. Dogs love to play and if you teach your dog by playing a game, you'll be much more successful.

7. Set your dog up for success. The fastest way to backfire your training is to call your dog as he is going in the opposite direction. That is a recipe for disaster.

So, there you have it, seven tips to get your dog coming back to you when you call.

And here's one more I like to call "The Parrothead Secret"

A couple of years back I went to see Eric Clapton in concert. I went with my wife and her sister and was really looking forward to it. Halfway through I couldn't wait for it to be over.

You see, I am a HUGE Jimmy Buffett fan. I have all his music on my phone. I have all his books and try to go to his concerts when he comes around. I am a true Parrothead. (Parrot Head or Parrothead is a commonly used nickname for fans of Jimmy Buffett.)

His concerts are an experience. From the second you pull into the parking lot it is one big, giant party that continues with Jimmy joining in from the stage. He interacts with the crowd, talks about the area, and has fun the whole time.

Eric Clapton walks on stage and technically is probably the best you'll ever hear. His band is also technically amazing. They can play, but to me it was just boring. I share this observation with you because it can help teach your dog to come when called.

Anyone can technically train their dog to come when called and most people do. They stand there and say, COME. Their dog trots over and a treat is dispensed. Teaching your dog to come when called and just handing your dog a treat will never develop the rocket-fast, reliable recall that you want.

You need to make it more of an experience for your dog. You need to use your tone of voice, your body language, movement, and high-powered rewards.

What's that? This all sounds like a lot of work? I know what you're saying but so is chasing your dog down the street on a cold morning with just your bathrobe on. So, here is a cheat sheet to help you out.

Come When Called Cheat Sheet

I never cheated on a test in school. I would have never been able to pull it off. I knew that I would have been caught so I usually failed most of my tests. To this day I don't know how I actually graduated from high school. Anyway, there is no test for teaching your dog to come when called and that is why I developed a simple cheat sheet that you can print, use, and share with your dog loving friends.

This cheat sheet gives you the main points for teaching your dog this important command. Here it is:

RECALL COMMAND CHEAT SHEET

1. Practice the recall command when your dog has a lot of energy.

2. Use the best, most high-powered treats you have.

3. Set your dog up for success using the Restrained Recall Exercise (full explanation earlier in chapter).

4. Use a combination of treats and games to teach your dog to come when called.

5. When your dog gets to you, always make sure you are holding onto the collar before you give the treat. This will avoid the keep away game that dogs love to play once they learn that when they get to you, you put them on leash.

6. Use a long line to influence your dog's behavior from a distance.

7. Use a long line to teach your dog to work through distractions.

8. Start with low distractions and work your way up to more and more difficult distractions.

9. Always make sure your dog is safe when you are outside.

I have been working with dogs for 40 years as an animal care specialist, veterinary assistant, and pet groomer. I have trained all my dogs with Eric Letendre since 1995 and he is one of the most skilled, patient, and kind dog trainers I have ever met. My Doberman, Remi, has progressed so much and is now on her way to being completely off-leash trained thanks to what we learned with Eric. At my pet grooming business, Pawlissa, we refer all our clients to Eric Letendre's Dog Training School in Westport MA.

PAULA ANDRADE

CHAPTER FIVE:
TEACHING SIT / DOWN / STAND

> *Eric is truly amazing. Over the past almost two years, he has shown us how to deal with our exuberant, happy, and often stubborn Charlie and help him become the great dog he is today. In May 2016 Charlie was out of control. By November 2017 he passed the American Kennel Club's Canine Good Citizen test and is still continuing with his training. If you have a chance to learn to train your dogs with him do it. Eric's training is the best you'll find.*

MARIE CONOLLY

"I don't like little kids in my dog training class!"

"And... NO TREATS! If I catch you giving your dog any treats, out you go! Every dog is required to use a choke chain for training." Standing there, looking up I thought, "This guy is scary."

I was ten years old and I was going to my first obedience class with our little family beagle named Union Park (I know what you're thinking. His dog is named Union Park? Yes, story for another day). Anyway, the obedience instructor was none too happy to have me in class and made it very clear.

The first command we were going to teach was the stay command. He instructed me to tell my dog to stay and walk to the end of the leash. I told her to stay, walked to the end of the leash, and she didn't budge... for two seconds. Then she ran to me and jumped up like she always did.

The instructor quickly stepped in and told me to "correct" her back into the sit-stay position. I did my best to get her back into position. I told her to stay, walked to the end of the leash, and she again ran over and jumped on me.

I was too nervous to look at the instructor. He told me to give him the leash. He yanked on the leash, roughly put her back into the stay position, and walked to the end of the leash. My Catholic training kicked in and I started a silent Hail Mary prayer, pleading for my little beagle to stay there and not get into trouble.

And... she broke the command and jumped on him. He turned to me and as I looked up into his eyes, I knew my dog and I were in hot water. The instructor's finger came within a few inches of my nose and he said:

"This dog had better do a perfect stay command by the time you come back next week," and then he tossed the leash to me as he stormed off.

Funny I decided to make a career of dog training when this was my first experience. So, I practiced all week and when we returned, I had accomplished the impossible. My little beagle could now do a very solid sit-stay command. I yanked on her little neck all week like I was taught. It took a lot of effort, but I got her to stay.

The following week we went back to class and I proudly showed the instructor how well my little beagle could now do a sit-stay command. He didn't seem too impressed. He turned to the class and informed us of the next command we were going to teach.

"Today we are teaching the recall command. Your dogs are going to learn to come to you when you call COME." The instructions were given. "Class, you are going to tell your dogs to stay. You are going to walk to the end of the leash. At the end of the leash you will call COME to your dog."

As instructed, I told my dog to stay, walked to the end of the leash, faced her, and clearly called COME! - COME! - COOOMMMEE!!!

She didn't move an inch. She was doing a perfect stay command. I could feel the instructor moving towards me. He looked down at me and asked what was wrong? I said she was staying there. He said...

"YANK THE LEASH!"

I share this story often in class because it explains how training a dog can be very confusing, not only for the owner, but also for the dog. This is why I work so hard to clear up the confusion for dog owners. A command as simple as sit and stay can turn into a disaster for the dog. The story I told you happened way back in the 1970's when The Brady Bunch and bell bottoms were popular, but unfortunately, in many places, dog training is still accomplished this way.

As your humble, hard-working dog training guide, helping you make sense of the murky and confusing world of dog training, I have put together a video explaining how to teach your dog the stationary commands.

https://www.youtube.com/watch?v=_C511MVs7m0

DEFINITION OF SIT

Our definition of SIT is to have the dog place his hind quarters on the ground when you give the verbal command SIT. The dog should do the command the first time you say it and continue doing it until released from the command with a YES. SIT should be performed with no physical help and regardless of distractions or location.

SIT is often looked at as a simple command and not much attention is given to it. SIT is a complex command when done properly. Refer to the video above if you are having trouble getting your dog into the sit position.

DEFINITION OF DOWN

Our definition of DOWN is to have the dog place his body on the ground when you give the verbal command DOWN. The dog should do the command the first time you say it and hold it until released from the command with a YES. DOWN should be performed with no physical help and regardless of distractions or location.

From a recent group training class:

Excellent, now let's move on to the down command. Down is a little more difficult but we are going to get your dog to do this command. When we teach down, we want our dogs to do the command the first time we say it and for as long as we want. The dog should not move until we release the dog.

Okay, I am going to start with the dog in a sit position and I am going to guide the dog into a DOWN. I hold the treat on the dog's nose and gently guide the dog towards the floor.

Do any of you notice anything while I do this?

YES! I am not saying down. I am doing that for a reason so let me explain. We always teach a command first and then we name it. You see, if your dog is struggling to get into a DOWN and you keep saying DOWN, what is the dog associating the command with? Let me give you an example. Let's say every time I say DOWN, the dog's butt goes up in the air. I say DOWN, butt goes in the air, DOWN, butt in the air, DOWN, butt in the air. What is the dog going to think DOWN means? Yes, you're right, he is going to think DOWN means butt in the air.

Now, once your dog starts to go DOWN every time you lure the dog into position, you can start to name it. We always teach the behavior and then we name the behavior. Does that make sense? Great! Go ahead and try it with your dog and I will come around to see how you are doing.

DEFINITION OF STAND COMMAND

Our definition of STAND is to have the dog in the STAND position when you give the verbal command STAND. The dog should do the command the first time you say it and do it until released from the command with a YES. STAND should be performed with no physical help and regardless of distractions or location.

From a recent group training class:

Alright, the last command we are going to teach is the STAND command. The good news is STAND is very easy to teach. The question I often get is, "Why are we teaching STAND? Why do we need to teach this?"

Stand is very important for a few different reasons. First, STAND is useful if you ever find yourself in a situation and you need your dog to stay still for a few seconds without moving but the conditions are not the best. If you were hiking on a muddy path and needed your dog to not move, STAND is the perfect command. You don't want your dog to DOWN or SIT in the mud, so STAND is perfect.

Another reason STAND is good is if your dog needs grooming or goes to the vet. If your dog can do a really good STAND, your groomer will be very happy with you. Same with the vet. It is easy to examine a dog in the STAND position.

And the last reason is we want your dog to learn commands, NOT patterns. A lot of dogs learn SIT and DOWN back to back. DOWN always follows SIT. So, the typical pattern is SIT, DOWN, SIT, DOWN, SIT, DOWN. After a few days of practice, your dog will start to DOWN after you give the SIT command. They anticipate the next command. STAND will mix things up for your dog. See, you want your dog to go from one command to the next. Your dog should be able to go from STAND to DOWN, from DOWN to STAND, from STAND to SIT and SIT to STAND. Does that make sense?

Okay, now I am going to demonstrate how to do a STAND command. You start by holding the treat right in front of the dog's nose and you guide him into a STAND position. We still must build duration - GOOD, and then release - YES. Okay, go ahead and try it out and I'll come around and see how you are doing.

When you practice this week, practice having your dog go from one command to the next in any order. Get your dog to learn how to do the commands without relying on the last command.

Alright, so what did we learn today? We went over SIT, DOWN, and STAND. Work on those commands and please let me know if you have any questions.

DOG TRAINING?
AIN'T NOBODY GOT TIME FOR THAT!

Can six words launch a career? It did for "Sweet Brown" Wilkins. If you don't know what I'm talking about, Sweet Brown was being interviewed by a news station after a fire in her apartment complex. The video has tens of millions of views. You can watch it here:

http://www.youtube.com/watch?v=udS-OcNtSWo

At the end of the interview she states: "Ain't nobody got time for that!"

I think that is why so many people connected with her. Everyone is so busy these days. One of the biggest complaints I hear is that people don't have time for anything extra - like dog training. As always, I am here to help.

Dog training does NOT require large blocks of time. In fact, you will get much better results by breaking up training into short five minute or less sessions. Here is a great dog training schedule for you to follow. The times will vary for you but here is what I do:

6:00AM Dog goes out to pee and poop. Quick set of SIT, DOWN, and STAND.

6:45AM Time for breakfast: 30-second SIT-STAY before meal.

7:30AM Before leaving for the day we go outside. Before going through the door, I have my dog do a DOWN-STAY. Once outside we practice a few recalls and finish with a few sets of SIT, DOWN, and STAND.

3:00PM Outside - after dog has relieved herself, we do a few RECALL COMMANDS. Once we come in the house, we work on a few tricks.

3:30PM Out for a walk. During the walk we'll do a few RECALLS, SIT, DOWN, STAND, STAY, and WALKING politely on leash.

4:00PM Back home and she does a few obedience commands for a treat.

6:00PM Dinner time. 45-second DOWN-STAY before meal.

You see how short each session is? Just a few minutes at a time. It is also incorporated into day-to-day activities. You get better results this way because your dog learns to listen to you throughout the day instead of just when you do a formal session.

Eric is an insightful and easy to work with trainer. He's helped us immensely to gain better control of our new JRT and make a good relationship with the dog even better. What I liked best about the sessions was the "hands on" aspect of the training - you actually get help implementing the methods, and you will see the results right there on the spot. The follow-up is all up to you, but I am now happy that I can have a well-behaved dog that people like to have around. The best part is Cosmo enjoys the training and seems to be even happier.

Highly recommend Eric to anyone looking for help with a challenging dog. He is effective, professional, and has a very pleasant working style which makes you and the dog feel comfortable and confident.

TONY DISALVO

CHAPTER SIX:

UNDERSTANDING PRESSURE AND RELEASE

I have been living with a very reactive Border Terrier for the past five years. I went to a training class in my area and got zero results. I had worked with Eric years ago in Newington, CT and finally being completely exasperated with my dog's behavior around other dogs, I made the two hour trip from Manchester, CT to see Eric at his dog training school in Westport, MA for a training session.

He told me he could help me in one 45-minute session. I was skeptical but he was right. In just one session (and in less than 45 minutes) he got my out control, barking, pulling on leash dog completely under control and calm around other dogs. I was truly amazed at how clearly and calmly he helped me teach my dog to behave around other dogs. If you're looking for the BEST dog trainer, go to Eric Letendre's Dog Training School in Westport, MA!

MARIA JOHNSON

LIGHT ON THE LEASH

"Light on the leash" is a term used by dog trainers to describe a dog who is very sensitive to the leash and walks with very little pulling. A dog who is "light on the leash" is a pleasure to walk and bring anywhere. In this chapter, I will explain how we are going to teach your dog to respond to the leash, so all your walks become enjoyable.

In our adult dog training program, during your first private dog training session, we cover two main components to dog training. We discuss communication and leash pressure. Pressure and release is crucial to dog training and when used properly, it can change the whole relationship you have with your dog. You'll be able to communicate on a much higher level and have a very responsive dog that listens to all your commands.

Teaching the "language" of leash pressure...

PRESSURE AND RELEASE

Everything in life is pressure and release. We constantly feel pressure to complete certain tasks. We often put off important tasks until the pressure becomes more intense. As I write this, April 15th is a few days away. Many of you automatically know what kind of pressure I am feeling. April 15th is the deadline for filing taxes. I waited until the pressure was strong enough to make time to sit down and get it done. As soon as I drop my returns in the mail, I will be released from the pressure of getting my taxes done until the next new pressure is upon me.

The concept of pressure and release is important for your dog to learn because most dogs would happily choose to ignore us when something better is out there, like when they are on the beach sniffing around and thinking about eating the dead fish they just discovered.

POSITIVE REINFORCEMENT HAS LIMITATIONS

What you'll discover as you train your dog is that positive reinforcement has its limitations. If all you had to do was take a bag of treats with you to the beach or out hiking to get your dog to come back to you, we wouldn't need to discuss pressure and release. The problem is that most dogs will ignore you and the treat you are offering when they are distracted. The positive reinforcement of chasing the squirrel is stronger than the treat in your hand.

Dog training can be confusing and there is a lot of dangerous and misleading information out there on this topic. In fact, anyone who tells you to JUST use positive reinforcement is giving you deadly advice which is why I wrote an entire book about it. *The Deadly Dog Training Myth* explains why this is dangerous advice for unsuspecting dog owners. (Available on Amazon.com.)

THE LEASH IS A COMMUNICATION TOOL

The leash is an important communication tool for training your dog. It is literally a lifeline attached to your dog to keep him safe and help teach obedience. Our goal is to help you train your dog to a high level of comfort every time you have the leash on your dog. No one likes to be dragged down the street or have a sore arm after every walk.

Leash pressure is taught through negative reinforcement. Negative reinforcement sounds bad until you learn how it really works. In fact, negative reinforcement is used on you daily to potentially save your life!

WHAT IS NEGATIVE REINFORCEMENT?

Negative reinforcement is used to compel you to DO A BEHAVIOR. This is important. We often think negative reinforcement STOPS a behavior. This is incorrect. Punishment stops a behavior. Reinforcement gives more of a behavior.

There are two types of reinforcement - Positive and Negative.

Negative reinforcement is commonly thought to inflict pain, but it can actually be applied without any contact to the person or dog it is being used on. A common example is the seat belt in your car. In the 1970's, car manufactures started to install an audio and visual system to put pressure on the driver to buckle up. A buzz or bell starts ringing and will not go away until you DO A BEHAVIOR. When you put your seatbelt on, the bell goes away.

This is a perfect example of pressure and release. It also has an important lesson about negative reinforcement. In your car, you are in control of the negative reinforcement. You can make that ringing go away whenever you want. You can drive for hours with the bell dinging, or you can stop it immediately by buckling up. This is IMPORTANT to remember as you train your dog using pressure and release. Your dog also controls negative reinforcement.

When you apply pressure to your dog it is important to watch your dog's response. The gentle training exercises we go over with you during our first session are designed for your dog to learn how to yield to leash pressure. They are also taught to help you learn when to apply and when to release pressure.

OPPOSITION REFLEX

If I was to put my hand on your shoulder and gently push into you, you would start to resist and push back. This is an example of opposition reflex. As I apply pressure you apply counter-pressure to keep your balance. Dogs feel the leash and they naturally apply pressure and resist. Every time your dog pulls, he is getting better at it.

We use the prong or slip collar to help your dog better understand where we want him to be as we walk. These tools also help him understand better than a harness or a flat collar.

The faster we help your dog understand what is expected of him, the less stress on your dog. The prong collar is one of the most humane collars for helping train dogs.

When we apply pressure through the leash, the collar will engage. This is done with light pressure. Remember, the goal is to use as little pressure as needed to get a response from your dog. Training a dog is NOT about heavy-handed FORCE. Training is about helping your dog learn to comply with the commands he needs to learn. As the pressure is applied, you want to watch your dog's response. At first, you are just looking for a few steps from him. When your dog takes a few steps with the pressure, release. The collar is DISENGAGED, and your dog is rewarded.

Use as little pressure as possible to get your dog to move.

This is why we have you practice leash pressure on our arm before we do it with your dog.

LEASH PRESSURE IS TAUGHT SEPARATELY FROM OBEDIENCE

During the first session, our focus will be on COMMUNICATION. We cover THE 4 MAGIC WORDS and LEASH PRESSURE.

Your homework for the first week is to continue to focus on communication and not obedience. Your dog will learn obedience commands much faster when he understands the communication system we are using.

At home, practice using THE 4 MAGIC WORDS and LEASH PRESSURE. Following are the exercises to work on with leash pressure.

*Remember, the leash is always parallel to floor. Do not pull up on the leash, always pull straight back or straight forward

EXERCISE #1: BACKING AWAY FROM THE TREAT
Hold a treat in front of your dog's nose. When your dog pulls toward the treat, apply pressure back. When your dog goes with the pressure, release the pressure and reward.

Remember, the leash should be almost parallel with the floor as we teach leash pressure. A common mistake is pulling up. You want to pull back or forward on the leash (depending on what exercise you are doing). Pulling up will result in your dog going in a direction we don't want him to at this time.

EXERCISE #2: MOVING FORWARD WITH LEASH PRESSURE
This is practiced along the side of a wall. (Wall, dog, human.) Gently pull your dog forward. When your dog moves forward, release the pressure and reward. Once your dog is doing good along the wall, switch sides. Then take him off the wall and try on both sides.

EXERCISE #3: MOVING BACKWARD WITH LEASH PRESSURE
Standing still against a wall, pull back on the leash. You want your dog to back up as you stand still. Once your dog moves backward, release pressure and reward.

EXERCISE #4: WALKING BACKWARD WITH LEASH PRESSURE

Along the wall, have your dog walk backwards with leash pressure. Pull straight back. You want your dog to walk backward with slight amounts of pressure. Keep doing it until your dog can back up the length of wall.

EXERCISE #5: ABOUT TURNS

In a straight line, start walking with your dog. When your dog gets in front of you, do a turn away from your dog and apply gentle, steady pressure until he moves towards you. Make sure you release pressure as your dog moves towards you.

HOW LONG BEFORE MY DOG LEARNS LEASH PRESSURE?

After four to five sessions, your dog should understand leash pressure. If you can practice leash pressure once a day between the initial private lesson and your first group class, your dog should understand leash pressure. Please let us know if you have any questions or problems.

SENSITIVE DOGS

If your dog is very sensitive, do shorter sessions with long breaks in between. Leash pressure is learned much faster than positive reinforcement. Positive reinforcement takes many repetitions for your dog to learn. Leash pressure is learned at a much faster pace, but you should still take your time.

STRESS AND YOUR DOG

There is stress with learning leash pressure. However, small amounts of stress are good for your dog. The U.S. Military has performed studies on exposing young puppies to small amounts of stress. In these studies, puppies as young as 2-weeks old are taken from the litter for very short periods of time and exposed to low level stressors, such as being placed on a cold towel for fifteen seconds before being returned to the litter.

These studies have found puppies exposed to low level stress are much better able to handle stress as they become adults. They exhibit lower heart rates and recover from stressful situations much faster such as exposure to fireworks and being left alone. Excessive stress is bad but learning to deal with low level stress is important for all dogs.

Only positive or all positive training tries to remove ALL stress from the training process and from the dog's life in general. This is EXTREMELY unhealthy for a dog because throughout his life, he will have to deal with stressful situations. Going to the veterinarian's office, the groomers, being left alone, experiencing thunderstorms, stays at boarding kennels, and travel are all stressful to a dog.

Our training program is designed and developed to help your dog become much more stable and able to handle all situations. Teaching leash pressure is a great way to teach your dog to cope with stress.

LEASH WALKING

Start walking with your dog. If your dog starts to pull, apply pressure and walk backwards, guiding your dog back to you and then start moving forward again. Your dog will do a quick U-turn at your side once you start moving forward again.

BLOCKING

This is giving your dog light leash pops to teach him to "hold himself" before he is allowed to do what he wants. Leash pops are used more as guidance than punishment. Some examples where this would be appropriate would be:

- Going through doors
- Approaching another dog
- Approaching a person
- Pulling towards fire hydrants, etc.

Follow the steps in this chapter and your dog will understand leash pressure in no time. The great news is your dog will be MUCH, MUCH easier to walk and will listen to you better once he understands leash pressure.

I hope you are as excited as we are for your next training session. Over the course of this six-week program, your dog is going to learn loose leash walking, coming when called, sit, down, stand, stay, and the place command. We will also help eliminate any behavior problems you may be experiencing with your dog. And, your dog will be "Light on the Leash" in no time.

Thank you for choosing Eric Letendre's Dog Training School to help you train your dog. We look forward to seeing you and your dog at the next class.

> *Eric Letendre's Dog Training School in Westport, MA is the BEST place to go to train your dog. When we were looking for puppy training, my veterinarian told me to contact Eric and I am glad I did. Eric has helped us train our dog and she now walks perfectly on leash. We just started off-leash training and are excited to keep training with Eric.*
>
> *If you are looking for dog training, call Eric Letendre's Dog Training School and do the free consult. You and your dog will be as happy as I am. Thanks for all your help Eric!*

RUI & AMY CANITO

CHAPTER SEVEN:

HOW TO WALK ANYWHERE, ANYTIME, ANYPLACE, AROUND ANY DISTRACTION

Just a few short months ago, John and I were stressed taking our three Shepherds out for a walk. The three of them would pull us all over the place. It was not fun, and we didn't really want to walk them as it was so stressful. Thanks to Eric Letendre's Dog Training School, in just a short time we have them working together and one or the other of us can take all three of them for walks now without any more pulling. Now we can enjoy our walks with them as much as they enjoy going out for a walk. Thank you, Eric, ever so much!

MARLENA MANCHESTER

DEFINITION OF HEEL

Our definition of HEEL is to have the dog walk at the owner's side. Perfect HEEL position is when the back of the dog's paw is in line with the back of the owner's heel. There are four behaviors the dog is NOT allowed to do when HEELING:

1. NO PULLING
2. NO BITING THE LEASH
3. NO BARKING
4. NO SNIFFING

When the owner comes to a stop, the dog should remain at their side until released from the command.

DOES YOUR DOG DRAG YOU DOWN THE STREET?

I had a lady walk into my office once with two huge black eyes. She sat down and started to cry. I thought she was just assaulted and was getting ready to call the cops. Come to find out she was crying because of her dog. Her dog was a big, happy lab that was very strong and gave her the black eyes.

She was getting ready to walk her dog when she stopped as she was walking out the door. Her dog was outside, but she was still inside the house. The dog saw a cat and immediately took chase. She held onto the leash and went face first into the door.

She told me that this was not the first time her dog had injured her, that he was so strong and if she could not get him under control she would have to find him a new home. That's when I taught her the secret to loose leash walking.

And I'm going to share it with you.

I can share it in two words: *Opposition reflex.*

That's a fancy term that simple means this: Whenever you apply pressure, the dog will resist and apply counter-pressure.

Push your dog into a down and the dog will resist. Try pushing your dog into a sit and most will push back. Attach a leash and when your dog feels you pulling back your dog will resist and pull forward.

The secret to loose leash walking is to NOT trigger your dog's opposition reflex. I know, it's easier said than done, and that is why I recommend certain tools when you first start training your dog to walk on leash. It is also why I don't use choke collars. In order for a choke collar to work, you have to learn how to yank it so it does not get tight.

So as you see, loose leash walking can take a little work to learn how to do it correctly. The good news is you are going to learn how to get your dog to walk with you, no pulling, and no out of control behavior.

You will have a nice calm dog you can take anywhere.

Eric is amazing! We have a Bernese Mountain Dog and have completed other training classes prior to enrolling in Eric's course, but none of them had worked. The first time we met with Eric, we were blown away at how knowledgeable he was. He's personable and has a great teaching style that works! Our dog, Murphy, learned more in the first 45 minutes spent with Eric than in all of his other previous puppy classes combined.

The biggest thing we were struggling with was Murphy pulling too hard on the leash when we walked him. This is common for Berners and since they grow really fast, it almost became too difficult to walk him at all. After just one class with Eric, Murphy's behavior improved significantly and now we are able to enjoy calm, peaceful walks that we initially never thought were possible. We would recommend Eric to anyone who has a dog and is interesting in teaching basic commands and especially to those who are struggling with breaking bad behavior with their dog. Thank you, Eric!!!

MICHAELA CAIZZI

Here are step-by-step instructions for teaching the HEEL command:

From a recent group training class:

Today we are going to be teaching your dog the HEEL command. HEEL is very important because your dog must be calm and controlled on leash. You need to bring your dog to the vet, groomer, daycare, or boarding kennel. You want your dog to be under your control in these situations. You should also try to walk your dog a minimum of four times a week. Walking provides mental and physical stimulation for your dog. The mental stimulation of the walk is extremely important.

Okay, there are two walking commands I teach a dog. I like to teach an informal LET'S GO command and I also like to teach a formal HEEL command. Tonight, we are going to focus on HEEL. Let me give you a quick explanation of the two. If I was walking on the beach with my dog I would say, LET'S GO, and let the dog do what she wants without pulling me. The dog can sniff, walk on my right side, my left side, I really don't care. It is a relaxed, informal walk. So, your dog can move along with you and do what they want as long as they are not pulling you.

The HEEL command is different. This is when I want your dog to move right at your side, paying attention, and I have four requirements for the dog when I am doing HEEL. Here they are:

FIRST, there is NO pulling, SECOND, NO barking, THIRD, NO biting the leash, and FOURTH, there is NO sniffing. We are going to allow your dog to sniff but it will be on your terms, not the dog's. Remember, the dog always lives ON YOUR TERMS.

Before we can start teaching HEEL. we must know where the HEEL position is. Does anyone know where HEEL is?

You say left side, you say right side, what is the correct side? The answer? There is no correct side. You can walk your dog on the right or left when you say HEEL. UNLESS... you are going to do competitive obedience. If you are going to compete with your dog and get a Companion Dog Title or more, then you must have your dog HEEL on your left side.

Here's the deal. I tell people to teach HEEL on your non-dominant side. If you are a right-handed person, have your dog HEEL on your left side. If you are a lefty, have your dog HEEL on your right side. See, most dog training comes from gun dog training, hunting dogs. Most people are right-handed, so the shotgun was in the right hand and the dog was on the left side. I am right-handed so my car keys are in my right pocket, I keep my cell phone in my back-right pocket. So, my right hand is free and my left hand is holding the leash. Does that make sense to everyone?

I want everyone to choose a side. When you say HEEL, your dog is going to be on the left or the right. Did everyone choose a side? Good, what side?

Great, now that everyone has a side we are going to go for a little walk. I want to see is how your dogs walk on leash with you. This is not a test, I don't care how your dogs behave, I don't care if they pull, I just want to get an idea of where we are with walking.

Okay, we are going to follow Mary and Sparky. Everyone is going to go in this direction. When I say forward, start walking. When I say stop, come to a stop and sit your dog. If I say about turn, turn 180 degrees and go the other way. Ready? Forward. Good, good, okay stop.

Excellent. You guys did great. I noticed a few of the dogs were still pulling a little even with the prong collar on. So, let's fix that. Here are a couple of things you must understand about walking a dog on a leash. Have any of you ever heard of opposition reflex? Opposition reflex is interesting. It basically works this way. As you apply pressure to the dog, the dog resists the pressure. Think of it this way. If I push on your shoulder, you feel my push and start to resist the pressure I am applying. Have any of you ever tried to push your dog into a down position? You push down and your dog resists and pushes back. The same happens when you have a dog on leash. You pull back on the leash and your dog resists. So, the trick to walking a dog on a loose leash is to make sure there is ZERO tension in the leash.

So, the first step to loose leash walking is making sure you are relaxed. You are not pulling on the leash, creating opposition reflex. The second step is to make sure the prong collar is disengaged. Let's start with the first step. The first step is to hold the leash correctly. You must be relaxed as you hold the leash. If I asked everyone to stand up and stand there and relax, everyone would stand like this... (demonstrate a relaxed stance.) You would stand with your arms relaxed at your side. Your elbows would not be bent, your hands would be at your side facing behind you. Your hands would not be facing forward like this (stand with your hands facing forward).

I am showing you this because this is how you want to hold the leash. You hold the leash the same way you would as you were standing in a relaxed manner. You first take the leash, the loop at the end of the leash, and put your thumb through the loop and then make a fist like this:

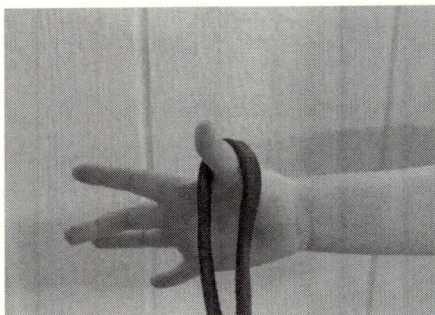

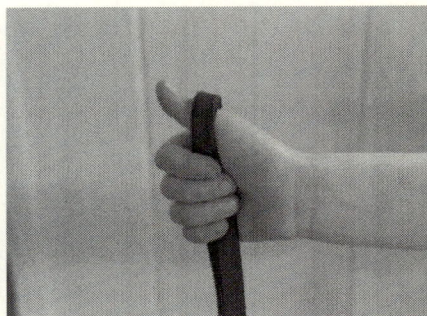

With your other hand you are going to use what we call an overhand grip. You have an overhand grip and an underhand grip. We use different grips for different situations, for leash walking, we use an OVERHAND GRIP. An underhand grip is holding the leash with the palm of your hand facing the ceiling an overhand grip your palm is facing the ground. We want to use an OVERHAND GRIP.

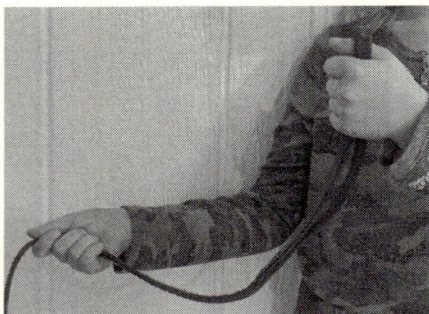

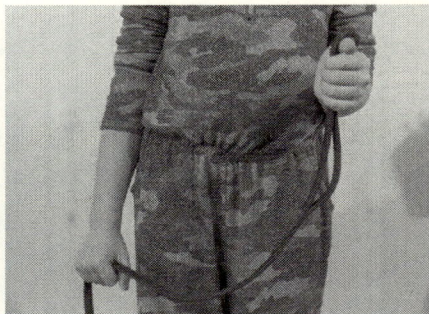

Underhand Grip   Overhand Grip

Remember when I demonstrated standing here relaxed, my hands were at my side like this. This is a relaxed grip. If I use an underhand grip, look what happens to my elbows (see above picture on left). I naturally bend them.

Guess what happens when I bend my elbows. Yes, I pull up on the leash. When I pull up on the leash look at what happens to the collar. Yes, I engage the collar. What happens when I engage the collar? Yes, I create opposition reflex and when there is opposition reflex, your dog is going to pull. You see why it is so important to hold the leash correctly and RELAX!

The prong collar is such a wonderful training tool because it allows us to be very gentle in our training. It allows us to communicate without using a lot of force and helps clear up the confusion. Here is what you must understand, this collar should be disengaged 99% of the time you are walking your dog. If the collar is engaged, your dog will pull unless they are extremely sensitive to the collar. So always keep the collar disengaged.

Okay, now that you know how to hold the leash, we are going to do some walking again. I want everyone to hold the leash the way I showed them and we are going to follow Mary and Sparky again. Remember, when I say forward, everyone starts walking, about turn, 180 degrees in the other direction and stop. Ready... forward.

Excellent, everyone can take a seat. Did you notice some of your dogs were still pulling a little? They did great but some of them were still pulling and you were holding them back more than the dog walking at your side with zero tension. So, let's fix that problem. Here is what you must understand about leash walking. You must think of leash walking like boundary training. Is everyone here familiar with or heard of Invisible Fence? Invisible Fence is an underground fencing system and when the dog leaves the yard (crosses the invisible fence), the collar activates and the dog learns to stay in the yard. It's a very effective system.

Invisible Fence works by letting the dog know they are close to the boundary. The collar beeps and if the dog continues, the collar gives a correction. Within a few repetitions the dog learns to stop moving forward when they hear the beep. We want the same thing to happen when we are walking. Imagine an invisible barrier about six to seven inches off your thigh.

I want the dog to stay behind this boundary as we walk. If the dog approaches the boundary, I give a little warning. I like to say "EHH" as the dog gets close. If the dog passes the boundary, I give a quick short pop with the leash in a backward motion. I want to pop the leash back like this. This can be done gently because your dog has been conditioned to the collar. You can give a couple of quick, short pops to get your dog behind the boundary. As you practice, you'll see your dog learn to stay next to you.

You see, the prong collar should not be engaged while you walk. If you are walking with the collar engaged, your dog will resist. Your dog can develop a tolerance to the prong collar and pull. This is why it is so crucial for the collar to be disengaged as you are walking. Here let me show what I mean.

Okay, let me show you. Can I use Sparky? See how Sparky is pulling? As I start walking and Sparky puts some tension into the leash, I give a quick pop back like this and see how Sparky stays right next to me? That is what you are going to do. Okay, let's stand up and try this out.

The reason we need the dog next to us is because we want the dog to see our leg as we are moving. The dog needs to pay attention to us and move with us. If we speed up, slow down, stop, turn, the dog needs to do it with us. If I was standing next to this pole, I can see it from this position. If I take one step forward, I can no longer see it.

Let's try it again.

Excellent, everyone is doing great. Now we are going to talk about getting rid of the prong collar. A question I get often is, "When can I stop using the prong collar?" My answer is: "When the dog tells you." You see, my goal is to get the dog working without any tools. I want the dog to listen to my verbal commands with no use of tools or treats. I want the dog to perform the command. That is my end goal when training a dog. But we need to use the tools until we build up enough repetitions to the point where the dog really understands the command.

So, at this point, I like to take my hands off the leash. By taking my hands off the leash I can see how the dog is progressing. Does the dog understand he is supposed to walk next to me? Does the dog listen to just my voice command? If he does, I am getting closer and closer to using the tools less and less. See, my ultimate goal is to get the dog off-leash trained where I can just use my voice to get the dog to perform the command. Does that make sense?

Okay we are going to go hands-free. Now remember, I said hands-free, NOT leash-free. You are going to keep the leash on, but your hands are coming off the leash. We do this by draping the leash over our shoulders. This allows us to take our hands off the leash, but we can still control the dog if we need to. We start by walking the dog with our hands off and see if the dog will respond to just our voice. If the dog does not respond we can grab the leash and influence the dog's behavior.

Okay, can I use Sparky? Thank you. I am going to drape the leash over my shoulders like this and start walking. Ready Sparky? Okay, "HEEL." Good Sparky. As I walk, I am trying to keep Sparky at my side. If he goes too fast, I will say EHH and help him back into position if I have to with a quick leash pop.

Alright, you guys ready to do it? Let's stand up and get our dogs ready. Have your dogs sit at your side. Drape the leash over your shoulders. Don't be nervous, if you need to, just reach down and grab the leash. If you are nervous just hold onto the leash as you walk. Ready? Forward.

And that is how you can eventually get your dog to walk without the prong collar. You keep practicing until your dog walks politely at your side with zero pulling. Everyone did great. Are there any questions? I'll be here if you do have any questions. Thanks so much for coming and everyone did great. Great group of dogs. You guys are doing a great job training your dogs. Keep up the great work. Thanks again!

How to Walk Anywhere, Anytime, Anyplace, Around Any Distraction

My goal is to help you train your dog to the point where you can take him as many places as possible. I also want you to always enjoy taking your dog for a walk. Teaching your dog to HEEL is one of the most important commands to teach.

Here are some points to keep in mind:

- When starting out, you must take the dog's age into consideration. Foundational training should be mostly positive, reward based. Puppy brains are not fully developed and do not have the mental capacity to focus and learn like a more mature dog.

- In the early stages, use the dog's meal. Most dogs are motivated to work for food.

- You need to shape the behavior before ever using a prong collar. Don't use prong collars on dogs under five months old.

- Leash handling and grip are important. Make sure you are using a thumb lock. Loop the leash again over your thumb to shorten the leash.

- You need to shape the habit of heeling and stop the habit of pulling. Use a gentle leader with puppies.

HOW TO TEACH THE HEEL POSITION

You are going to start by stepping forward and reversing direction on the dog. There is a good chance your dog is going to dart out in front. When they do, turn in the other direction and call the dog to follow you.

At this stage, try to avoid leash corrections. You want to let your dog know they should follow you. As the dog is behind you, mark the behavior "YES" and put a treat on the ground right next to your heel and take a step forward.

Repeat.

You want the dog to anticipate the treat getting put on the floor. Your dog will grab the treat and by the time they pick up their head, you are stepping forward and putting another one on the floor.

If the dog blows past you, change directions and repeat. Once your dog is doing well (five to ten rewards in a row) we can start to add duration. Add in a little bit of time between rewards. Walk a few more steps before putting the next treat on the ground. Only go one to two extra steps. Don't go for too long at first.

Continue to add duration and make longer and longer stretches (steps) between rewards. If your dog goes past you, use the non-reward marker WRONG and change directions.

We expect the dog to pay attention. Then come to stop, have your dog sit, and release them with YES! Always give the HEEL command after a break.

Start Adding Sit While in Heel Command

Take one step, stop, and give the command sit. Your right hand is the anchor, your left hand is the active hand which delivers treats.

Your left hand can either have an overhand or underhand grip. Remember, we want to use an OVERHAND GRIP.

Active and Passive Release of Pressure

Passive release requires the dog to move towards the owner to release pressure. This is kind of like a dog tied to a tree. The dog must do all the work in passive release.

Active release is when we take some action to relieve pressure from the leash. A slight pull towards us helps release pressure. The moment we feel them stop pulling we can give some relaxation to the leash.

Introduce the Prong Collar at this Point

With the prong collar on, we start changing directions on the dog. We want the dog to start following the owner.

Apply pressure and release as the dog starts moving with you. Apply leash pressure in a horizontal direction – away from the dog. Do short, mini sessions with the dog in the beginning using pressure and release while changing directions.

Use a minimal amount of pressure so the dog can be engaged and think about what he's doing. If you use too much pressure, thinking starts to shut down. You can use a very light pressure, just with your use fingertips, when using a prong collar.

If there are a lot of smells, your dog may get easily distracted and you may have to wait longer with the pressure on the leash. A good point to remember is to keep pressure in the leash until they move towards you, then release pressure.

Use patience as opposed to power. The release of pressure is the reward.

Once your dog learns to move with you, we need to teach the dog to stop with you. Introduce the stop when you turn away from the dog. Turn away and take a few steps and then come to a stop as you are stepping with your left leg. This gives the dog time to slow down with you.

Your dog does not have to sit at first. We can add that later.

The Leash Pop

Give a quick pop and release to the leash as the dog starts to pull away from you. Add the pop after the dog has become good at getting the treat placed on the floor next to you.

So, as you walk along, you put the treat on the floor next to you. When you go into the turn, say HEEL and give a quick pop on the leash. Then immediately say YES and put treat on the floor. Repeat.

HEEL is like a boundary training exercise. With Invisible Fence, the flags indicate where the dog is going to be corrected. The flags are the boundary, they are not to be crossed. It is a big mistake to wait until the dog is out in front and then correct. The flags are a visual reference of where the correction is going to happen. We want to correct our dogs at our hip. Our hip and leg become our visual cue for where the dog is to stay while walking. Dog should get a pop just as they pass the hip and leg. Behind our leg things are comfortable. As they drift in front, that is where they get the correction.

Relax and walk with a purpose. When you come to a stop, give the dog a little pop on the leash as you are coming to a stop. Do this when you think your dog is not going to stop with you. Try not to say SIT when you come to a stop. We want it to be automatic. Stop with your left foot forward, have your dog sit, and then bring other foot forward.

When using punishment, we want the dog to know what the punishment is for and how to avoid the punishment. The severity must be appropriate. The punishment should be enough to stop the behavior but not overwhelm the dog. It must be used for something the dog is actually capable of doing.

Stopping and Starting

This is an excellent drill to practice teaching your dog to pay attention to your left leg. It is also great for corrections for distractions. If a firmer correction is needed, it is good to practice doing stopping and starting drills.

As you come to a stop, take one step with your left foot while leaning back on your right foot and apply a firmer correction. Apply firmer corrections in the context of starting and stopping. This will help the dog understand the reason for the correction. Confusion on your dog's part leads to stress. We are always trying to communicate clearly what we want from our dog.

Practice coming to a stop by stepping forward with your left foot forward and right foot behind you. This is a que for the dog to come to a stop. Your dog does not have to sit at this point. Your dog will learn to sit when the right leg and left leg come together as you slow down.

About Turn

The about turn is one of the best ways to teach the dog to be more attentive to you. Your dog gets a harder correction doing the about turn. This is a very good exercise for strong distractions. The great thing with about turns is that the dog thinks they caused the correction. The correction is not associated with the handler. Footwork is important when doing this exercise. Don't walk in a big half circle. Walk forward, plant your left foot and make a quick turn to go in the opposite direction.

Your anchor hand stays right next to your belly. You can hook a thumb in your belt loop or pocket to help keep that anchor hand there. With the other hand, you are going to drop the leash, pivot, and turn away from the dog. Your left hand then takes the slack back in. There should be no hesitation while doing this exercise. No looking back. Do it as smoothly as possible.

I am amazed at the transformation and progress with my one-year old Great Dane. In just one class and one private lesson, we are certainly looking forward to the remainder of our classes. We are both in our 60's and this is our second Great Dane (I guess we were very lucky with our first and had no issues) We were unable to walk him, he was overpowering us, actually causing physical injury. Our goal is to walk comfortably and travel with him, and it upset us to know this was not happening. We met with Eric Letendre, he assured us that we could fix these issues, though hard for us to believe, we now had hope.

What an amazing transformation. We are so grateful to Eric for teaching us how to properly re-train our Otis. He is now 80% to a pleasant walking experience, and mind you, only two classes. We are now able to enjoy our Great Dane, all 120 lbs. of him, the way we should. I highly recommend Eric, he is professional, knowledgeable, kind and spot on! Thank you, Eric, for giving us the tools we needed to be able to enjoy our lovable, goofy boy, we can also see, he is a much happier dog!

JEANNE BERNARD

CHAPTER EIGHT:

HOW TO PARK YOUR DOG- TEACHING PLACE

> *I have a dog who is deaf. It was unbelievable what Eric was able to get her to do with hand signals after just ten minutes! I highly recommend him; you will not believe what he can get your dog to do!*

GEOFFREY CROTEAU

DEFINITION OF PLACE

Our definition of PLACE is to have the dog go, on command, to a bed (preferably raised). The dog is required to stay on the bed until released.

When I was 16 years old, I was shipped off to Boston. I had just failed my driver's test because I could not parallel park. I was going to spend the weekend with my Aunt Paulette. At the time, it was the worst thing to happen to me. But, by the time I left Boston, I could park a car anywhere.

My aunt had lived in Paris and was an expert at parallel parking. She taught me all her tricks. To this day I can park a car anywhere, from any side, on the busiest streets when the pressure is on.

This story came to mind as I was writing because in this chapter, I will show you how to teach your dog to GO TO PLACE. Your dog is going to learn how to get on his bed and stay there. Your dog will not come off the bed until you give permission. Pretty nifty little command to teach wouldn't you agree?

I often describe this as "Parking your dog." There are times you need to park your dog for a few minutes. Please don't get your panties in a bunch over the term. I once had someone tell me it is mean to "Park your dog."

Recently, I made a YouTube video where I "park" my dog Skye for a few minutes while I vacuum my car. It's much better to park and keep them safe then let them run around when it is not safe. Anyway, in this chapter I break it down step-by-step.

From a recent group training class:

Today we are going to be teaching your dogs the PLACE command. This is a great command to teach your dogs. This command is very helpful in so many different situations. One thing about having a dog is knowing what they are doing. In busy situations, PLACE allows you to park your dogs for a few minutes. If there are kids running around, if the front door opens, if a friend of yours is nervous around dogs, PLACE is used in these situations.

PLACE is also great for teaching your dogs duration. Remember, we want your dogs to maintain whatever command you give until released. So, if you give your dogs the command DOWN, we want your dogs to remain in the down position until you say YES! and release them. This is a difficult concept for your dogs to learn and understand. If I asked you to have your dogs SIT right now, then asked you to walk out of the room, how many of your dogs would not move?

Right. Most, if not all your dogs would not hold the command. They would not maintain the behavior which is what we need to teach them. The PLACE command is where I start teaching duration because having your dogs hold the command on the bed is easier for the dogs to understand. See, by having your dogs up on the beds, they quickly learn they are NOT supposed to come off the beds. The beds actually become an incredible learning aid. It helps the dogs learn much faster than without them.

So, I always teach duration on the bed and then I start to practice off the bed once the dog has a really good understanding of PLACE. Does this make sense to everyone? Does anyone have any questions? Okay great. Another reason PLACE is such a great command to teach is because it will help your dogs learn to be calm on command. You see, once your dogs get on the beds, we teach them they can't come off until we give permission with YES!. Once your dogs learn they can't come off without your permission, they will start to relax. If they know they can't come off the beds they may as well relax and be calm. This is a great command for easily overstimulated dogs.

The first step is to get your dogs comfortable with going on the beds. Some dogs will resist getting on the beds, so another reason for teaching this command is to build confidence. The first thing I always do is put a few treats on the bed and see if the dog will get on without any help from me. If he does, great. I will also take a treat and have him follow it up on the bed. It is important at this point that you do NOT say PLACE. You just want your dog to get up on the bed.

The reason we do NOT want to say PLACE is because if your dog resists getting on the bed or jumps to the side, your dog is making the wrong association with the command. Think about it, you say PLACE and your dog resists getting on the bed. Or you say PLACE and your dog jumps to the side. PLACE and your dog jumps to the side, PLACE and your dog jumps to the side. What is your dog learning? YES! Your dog is learning PLACE means jump to the side. So, at this point we don't want to say anything, we just want your dogs to get on the beds. Here, let me show you.

Okay, now you go ahead and try it with your dogs. I'll come around and see how you are doing.

Excellent, now that your dogs are getting up on the beds, we are going to add the next step. Now we are going to say the command right as your dogs are about to get on the beds.

You walk your dog up to the bed, right before your dog steps up on the bed you say PLACE. Once your dog is on the bed you are going to ask for a simple command... SIT. Once your dog is in the sit position, we are going to get a little duration. You are going to say GOOD, GOOD, and then YES! and have your dog come off the bed.

See, now we want your dog to start doing the command and staying on the bed for a few seconds. This is the beginning of having your dog learning to stay on the bed. The reason PLACE is such a great command to teach is it helps the dog understand duration better than anything else you can do. Your dog is up on the bed and he quickly learns he is supposed to stay on the bed. Go ahead and try this with your dog and I'll come around and see how you are doing.

Once your dog is doing this, we will see if we can start to work on longer duration. The great thing about teaching PLACE is your dog will go from five-second duration commands to two-minute duration commands. It really is quite amazing. This time you are going to walk up to the bed and say PLACE. Once your dog is on the bed, you are going to keep him there until I give you permission to let him come off. We are doing this as a group exercise. The dogs are going to stay on the beds until I say YES!. Everyone ready to try this? Great, now before we do this exercise what are you going to do if your dog comes off the bed?

If your dog starts to get off the bed, you are going to apply a little pressure to keep him on the bed. Your dog starts to step off the bed you are going to say WRONG and put a little pressure into the leash and get your dog back on the bed. We do this to teach the dog to stay on the bed for longer and longer periods of time. Your dog will start to learn to stay on the bed.

Okay, ready. All dogs on PLACE. Now, don't let your dogs come off the beds until I say so. If they do, give a little pressure to keep them on.

Excellent. That is what you want to do. You want to see if your dog can go longer and longer. I do up to an hour with my dog, Skye. It still amazes me how fast a dog can learn how to do this. The next step is to challenge your dog a little. You want to start putting a little distance between you and your dog. You want to see if you can go longer and add a few distractions. I will drop treats in front of Skye, I will toss a ball past her, or squeak a toy.

This time we are going to get our dogs on PLACE and challenge them a little. We are going to do this as a group and I am going to time it. If your dog starts to get off the bed, apply a little pressure to keep him on the bed. Ready? Go ahead and get your dogs on PLACE.

Alright, everyone is doing great. So, you want to keep doing this with your dogs and help them learn how to do duration commands on the bed. Once you think your dog is getting good with duration on the bed, you can start to practice off the bed on the floor. The last step for teaching PLACE is having the dog learn to go to the bed without any help from you. If you are standing here, and the bed's over there, you want to be able to tell your dog PLACE and have your dog leave you and run over and get on the bed.

This can be difficult for a dog to learn. The dog must walk away from you which is very different for your dog. Your dog is always moving to you, not away from you. We always call the dog to us. We never command the dog to move away from us. And dogs are extremely social. They want to be close to us.

But this is easy to teach because we use the right motivation. The way to do this is simple. You see, you want to put a treat on the bed and send your dog to go get the treat. There are a couple of ways to do this. You can step a foot or two away from the bed. You hold your dog by his flat collar and toss the treat on the bed. You want your dog to see the treat being tossed on the bed while you hold him back. You would then tell your dog PLACE and let go of the collar. Your dog will run over and get on the bed. Excellent. You then step in and praise your dog.

You need to be careful of grabbing the prong collar because if your dog tries to go for the treat and you give a correction your dog will not go when you say PLACE because he received the correction. Does that make sense? Let me show you.

Okay, excellent. Everyone is doing a great job. Everything we did today will do so much to help your dog learn PLACE. Remember, PLACE is great for learning duration, to help your dog become calm on command, and sometimes you just need to park your dog for a few minutes. This is where PLACE is great. So, practice PLACE and please let me know if you have any questions or concerns. Everyone did great tonight!

My miniature poodle and I just completed a Leash Walking course taught by Eric. Within four weeks, Halsey is now walking at heel with no more pulling. Walking is now fun and no longer stressful and annoying. Eric is knowledgeable, positive, and easy to work with. I highly recommend his classes and his individual training.

RENEE DAMGAARD

CHAPTER NINE:

HOW TO HOUSETRAIN YOUR PUPPY IN TEN DAYS OR LESS

Housetraining is a big problem for many puppy owners. To successfully housetrain your puppy, you only need to follow the next three steps:

1. Manage the behavior
2. Teach your puppy where it is acceptable and where it is unacceptable to go
3. Proper cleaning

STEP ONE: MANAGE THE BEHAVIOR

Management of behavior is extremely important when you are housetraining a puppy. Management simply means keeping a close watch over your pup's behavior. Most of the time, puppies will relieve themselves when we are not watching closely. Have you ever turned your back for a second only to discover your pup has urinated on your carpet? Happens all the time. Here is my first rule of thumb for puppy owners.

<u>Never, ever let your puppy out of your sight until he is completely house trained.</u>

Many puppy owners will ask me at this point: "What do I do when I cannot watch him?" My answer is still to manage the behavior.

A great management tool is the crate.

At some point in your dog's life there is a strong chance he will be required to go in a crate. If your dog ever must travel, go to a groomer, or spend the night at a vet's office, your dog will be placed in a crate. It is much better for him to learn crate training in the comfort of his home than to have some stranger shoving and forcing him into one when he is already probably stressed.

A crate is a great way to manage your puppy's behavior when you cannot watch him. Most puppies will not mess in the crate (if he does mess in the crate, I will discuss what you can do later on in this chapter) and it allows you to teach housetraining much faster.

One of the other reasons that I feel so strongly about crates is that I have seen plenty of dogs get injured when they were allowed too much freedom. I worked as an animal control officer for three years and during that time I saw dogs choke on objects, chew through electrical cords, get caught on fencing, and much more. Some of the dogs were only slightly injured. Some died. All the injuries could have been avoided with proper crate training and management.

HOW TO TEACH YOUR PUPPY TO LOVE THE CRATE

Some puppies do not like the crate. What most of them don't like is the separation from you. What we don't want to do is force your puppy into the crate. We want to teach him that the crate is a good place, a fun place, and a place he willingly enters. We want to teach your puppy to go to the crate on command. How do we do that? Simple. We develop his desire to go into the crate. Here is what you need:

- Kong toy
- Hot dogs
- String cheese
- Peanut butter
- Assorted treats

Put all the above on a table. Have your puppy's crate close by. Now call him over and pick up the Kong toy. With him right in front of you, show him the hot dogs as you put them in the Kong. Let him smell them but don't give him any. Now pick up the cheese and put some in the Kong. Then pack in a little peanut butter. Now take some of the assorted treats and stuff them in there. Take a little more peanut butter and top it off. Remember, I want you to do this with your dog watching; in fact, I want you to do this inches away from his nose. Now with your puppy still watching, take the Kong and toss it into the crate.

Here's the important part: Close the door on the crate but don't let your dog go in just yet.

Remember, I said that we wanted to develop his desire to go into the crate. If you have done everything correctly, your puppy should be outside of the crate looking in at the ultimate stuffed Kong toy. He should be pawing at the door. I want you to wait a few seconds and then I want you to take your hand off the door and tell him, "In the crate". At that point your puppy should open the crate door and grab the Kong.

DO NOT SHUT THE CRATE DOOR!

Let your pup grab the Kong and take it out of the crate if he wants. After doing this a few times, take a piece of string and tie it around the Kong toy and the crate so you dog cannot take the Kong out of the crate. Now he must stay in there to chew on the toy.

Only after your puppy starts to get comfortable in the crate should you start to close the door. Close the door for short periods of time. The first time you close the crate door, don't latch it. If your pup paws at it, it should open. Once he has been in for short periods of time, you can start to latch it for a few seconds and then minutes.

Another good thing to do is to start feeding your puppy all his meals inside the crate. When it is breakfast or dinner, put the food dish in the back of his crate.

Now that we have your puppy crate trained, you can start to use it when you cannot keep a close eye on his behavior.

The other reason that I am a big fan of crates is many times we will punish our dogs long after the behavior has occurred. If your puppy urinated on the carpet before you got home and you punish him for the accident, maybe as much as an hour after the behavior occurred, he will start to get confused.

It is important to remember when you are rewarding a behavior you have about one to three seconds to reward. If it takes you more than three seconds, there is a good chance he will think he is being rewarded for something else. No one would ask their dog to do a command like sit, walk away, come back 20 minutes later with a treat and expect the dog to understand the treat was for the sit he performed 20 minutes earlier. The same holds true with punishment. Why would we think our dogs would understand the punishment when we administer it long after the behavior has occurred?

Here is the other problem with too much punishment when we are housetraining puppies. The pup becomes afraid to go when we are around. I often get calls from dog owners who tell me they bring their dogs outside and stand around for hours and their dogs will not go. They come in the house and their dogs will not go. They know their dogs must go but they hold it. Then when they take their eyes off their dogs for just a second the dogs sneak off somewhere and go.

When I ask the dog owners what method of housetraining they have tried most of them explain they pushed their dog's nose into the mess or they gave them a good smack.

<u>Here's the problem:</u>

When you use heavy punishment to housetrain, your puppy learns to not go in your presence. When you are around, they "hold it" until they think you are not watching. Housetraining is a normal, natural function. Your job is to teach your puppy where it is acceptable to go. This can be accomplished by following the next step.

STEP 2: TEACHING YOUR DOG WHERE IT IS ACCEPTABLE

So now you're keeping a close eye on your puppy, you're putting him in the crate when you can't watch him. Now he needs to learn where he can go.

If your pup does start to go inside the house the best thing to do is to startle him. A loud "Hey" or "AH" is good. I usually will loudly clap my hands or stomp my foot and say, "HEY". I want to do it just firm enough to stop him. I then quickly put him on leash and take him outside.

One of the biggest mistakes puppy owners make is to tie the pup up outside or put him in a fenced in yard. **<u>You need to be right there with your puppy while you are housetraining</u>**. You see, training is all about influencing behavior. If your puppy is allowed to walk around without you there, then there is no feedback. You need to be right there to tell him, "Yes, this is where I want you to go." Bring your puppy to the same place in the yard on leash with some treats in your pocket. Once he is done, give him a reward.

HOW TO TEACH YOUR DOG TO "GO" ON COMMAND

This can be extremely useful, especially if you live in a cold part of the country. Standing outside waiting for your dog to go, wearing a bathrobe in sub-zero weather does not rank up there as one of the joys in life. Teaching your puppy to go on command is easy if you follow these steps.

1. Every time you bring him outside, he is on leash. While walking him, wait for him to give you the signals he is getting ready to go. Most dogs will sniff the ground, walk in circles, etc. After you have had your puppy for a while, you'll be able to tell. While he is giving the signals, start to say the command. I say: "Get busy". I'll keep saying it while he is sniffing the ground: "Get busy," "Get busy."

2. Once he starts to squat, stop talking. Let him finish before you say anything. If your puppy is going and you say in a high-pitched tone, "GOOD DOG," there is a good chance he will stop before he is completely finished.

3. The second he is done you can say: "GOOD DOG" and quickly reward with a treat. You want to strengthen and reward the behavior. I recommend using treats and praise.

If you follow these steps consistently, you will have a dog that goes on command. You'll be the envy of all your dog owning friends.

HOW TO TEACH YOUR DOG TO GIVE YOU A SIGNAL

When you are in the house it is a good idea to bring your puppy out before he is thinking about going. I get calls from dog owners that say their dogs do not give them any signals. I always recommend bringing your puppy out on a frequent schedule. Prevent the accident before it happens. Over a period of time, you will start to notice if your pup signals. Some will go to the door and scratch at it. Others will bark. Some, like mine, will pace. You need to keep a close eye on your puppy to see if he is trying to signal. If you see him sniffing the ground or circling, there is a good chance he is getting ready to go.

You can teach your puppy to give you a signal by hanging a bell from your door. Hang a small bell from your doorknob on a piece of string. Put a little peanut butter on the bell. When your puppy touches the bell, quickly open the door and bring him outside. Over time, he will learn touching the bell gets him outside.

STEP 3: CLEANING

A lot of housetraining problems start with the type of cleaning materials used. If the product contains any ammonia, it will smell like urine to your pup. If he smells the ammonia thinking it is the urine of another dog, he will try to cover the scent by going again in exactly same spot you just cleaned.

Cleaning should always be done with products that contain enzymes that can naturally break down the scent or vinegar and water. I like to use Nature's Miracle which can found in most pet stores.

COMMON PROBLEMS

Here are some typical questions that I get from puppy owners experiencing housetraining problems:

Q: I've tried a lot of what you suggest but I still seem to be having a problem. My puppy will urinate and defecate all the time. Is there anything I am missing?

A: When a puppy owner tells me their pup is going all of the time, I know this is not true. A dog can't go 24 hours a day, 7 days a week. He must stop some of the time. All kidding aside, if your puppy seems like he is always going, there is a good chance you are feeding him too much or too often. Most of the instructions on dog food bags advise to feed puppies three times a day. I recommend twice a day. You must remember what you put in will come out. Closely monitor how much food and water your pup gets for a few days and scale back a little. See if that makes a difference.

Q. My dog pees a lot. He drinks a lot and seems like he is always squatting and trying to go.

A. Sounds like you may have a physical problem, not a housetraining problem. I recommend getting a urine sample and having your vet check it. There is a good chance your pup may have a urinary tract infection.

Q. My dog goes in the crate. He doesn't care. He will urinate and defecate in the crate and just lay in it. I tried everything. What do you think I can do?

A. This is a big problem for some puppy owners. The first thing I would recommend is a vet check of your puppy's urine and stool to rule out any physical problem. The next thing I would advise is to get an x-pen.

When you are not there to watch your puppy, you can put him in the x-pen instead of the crate. The x-pen is large enough for your puppy to go in one area and then sleep in the other. When I am working with a puppy that will go in the crate I will either paper-train or I will teach him to go in a litter box. Now when you are home you will bring your puppy to the paper or litter box instead of taking him outside. When he goes on the paper or in the box you will reward every time. Now you can leave the paper or litter box in the x-pen for him when you are not there.

I know it is still a hassle, but it is better than giving a bath every day. Once he is successfully going in the litter box or on the paper, you can start to bring the litter box outside. If he goes to the litter box when it is outside, I would recommend leaving one out there for your puppy. Over a period of time you can wean him off the litter box or paper. Weaning is always a gradual process. With the paper you would start to make the area smaller and smaller.

Good Luck!

CHAPTER TEN:

ADDITIONAL RESOURCES

Thank you for choosing Eric Letendre's Dog Training School.

We have successfully helped thousands of dogs all over the South Coast, Rhode Island, and beyond.

We have put this book together to help you stay on track with your training. Everything we teach in the classes can be found in this book. This book can always be referenced to help answer any questions when you are training your dog.

In this book we also have links to videos you can watch to refresh your memory.

We are dedicated to doing everything we can to help you get the most out of our training programs. We are always available to answer questions. If at any time you have a question or problem, please contact us at 774-319-6351.

refeaf stop.

We do use an answering service so please be patient, but I will get back to you as soon as possible.

Thanks again and we look forward to helping you train your dog!

All the best!

Eric R. Letendre

We are very much interested in making sure you are successful training your dog. We are very active on social media and we provide a weekly email and updates. You can Like and Follow us on:

Facebook:
Facebook.com/EricLetendreDogTraining

YouTube:
YouTube.com/eletendre1

Weekly Email:
EricLetendre.com/e-newsletter

Books available on Amazon:
Amazon.com/-/e/B00A05KVLI

ABOUT THE AUTHOR:

ERIC R. LETENDRE

Since 1988, Eric Letendre has worked with and trained dogs from all angles. He is a former Fall River, MA Animal Control Officer, K-9 Supervisor, and has helped train dogs at most of the animal shelters in the area.

Eric is the author of four dog training books (available on Amazon) and has experienced and worked with every breed and behavior problem imaginable. Eric's popular YouTube channel has over 12 million views of its videos and he writes to thousands of dog owners all over the world through his popular weekly emails.

Knowing dog owners need fast and effective solutions, Eric has developed a training system anyone can follow. Based on a solid foundation of scientific training principles, it will train your dog to do more of the behaviors you want – sit, down, come, walk, etc. and STOP the behaviors you don't want – jumping, barking, chewing, etc.

Made in the USA
Middletown, DE
27 May 2023